# THE LAUGH BOOK

# THE LAUGH BOOK

## A New Treasury of Humor for Children

Compiled by
**Joanna Cole**
and
**Stephanie Calmenson**

Drawings by
**Marylin Hafner**

Doubleday & Company, Inc., Garden City, New York

Art direction by Diana Klemin.

Printed in the United States of America

Library of Congress Cataloging-in-Publication Data
Cole, Joanna.
 The laugh book.
 Includes index.
 Summary: A collection of jokes, riddles, tongue
twisters, tricks, games, poems, and stories.
 1. Children's literature. [1. Literature—
Collections. 2. Humorous stories. 3. Humorous
poetry]
I. Calmenson, Stephanie. II. Hafner, Marylin, ill.
III. Title.
PZ5.C7173La 1986 810'.8'09282 85–13113
ISBN 0-385-18559-6

9 8 7 6 5 4 3

# Acknowledgments

All possible care has been taken to make full acknowledgment in
every case where material is still in copyright. If errors have occurred, they will be corrected in subsequent editions if notification
is sent to the publisher. Grateful acknowledgment is made for permission to reprint the following:
Harry Allard. *It's So Nice to Have a Wolf Around the House* by Harry Allard and
illustrated by James Marshall. Copyright © 1977 by Harry Allard. Illustra-
tions copyright © 1977 by James Marshall. Reprinted by permission of
Doubleday & Company, Inc.
Richard Armour. "The Catsup Bottle" from *It All Started with Columbus,* re-
vised edition by Richard Armour. Copyright © 1961 by Richard Armour
and reprinted by permission of McGraw-Hill Book Company.
Judi Barrett. Excerpts adapted from *Cloudy with a Chance of Meatballs* by Judi
Barrett. Text copyright © 1978 by Judi Barrett. Reprinted by permission of
Atheneum Publishers, Inc.
Howard W. Bergerson. "Anagrams" are from *Palindromes and Anagrams* by
Howard W. Bergerson. Copyright © 1973 by Howard W. Bergerson and
reprinted with permission of the author.
Arthur Bloch. "Murphy's Laws" are from *Murphy's Laws* by Arthur Bloch.
Copyright © 1977 by Arthur Bloch. Used by permission of Price/Stern/
Sloan Publishing Inc.
Judy Blume. "Dribble!" is from *Tales of a Fourth Grade Nothing* by Judy Blume.
Illustrated by Roy Doty. Text copyright © 1972 by Judy Blume. Illustra-
tions © 1972 by E. P. Dutton. Reprinted by permission of the publisher,
E. P. Dutton, a division of New American Library.

THIS BOOK IS DEDICATED TO...

Rachel, JAIME, ERICA, BRIAN, Daniel, Jacqueline, Christopher, Jeffrey, MATTHEW, TODD, IMOGEN, JILL, michael, CHRISTIAN, BENJAMIN, ELIZABETH, Megan, Thea, Caffery, Emily, BETH, Patti, CHRIS, GARRETT, JHONEEN, CHRISTOPHER ANTHONY, Robby, TEDDY, Harris, & JANE!

NOT TO MENTION: Caroline, GEORGE LAURENCE, IRA, Spring, PETER, Lisa, Caleb, JOSIAH, & WILLOW.

We would like to thank the following people for their suggestions and support: Kermit and Edith Calmenson, Michael Calmenson, Marianne Carus, Lisa Castillo, Rachel Cole, Philip Cole, Ned Delaney, Daisy Edmondson, Madeleine Edmondson, Connie Epstein, Lynda Etkin, Jane and Jonathan Feder, Charlie Guettel, Ellen and Fred Guillermo, Stephen Manes, Dr. Charles Reasoner, Marilyn Sachs, Susan Schmeltz, Marjorie and Mitch Sharmat, Karen Stechel, Michael Stone, Elaine Thomas, Tony Vanaria, and Rachel Wilder.

Thanks also to these and other friends for telling us jokes and, more important, for listening to them.

# Contents

# • 4 •
# Laughing Gas
## *Funny Stories*

### • 5 •
## Row, Row, Row Your Goat
## *Funny Poems*
#### 243

## • 6 •
## Yours Till the Kitchen Sinks
### *Autographs*
269

## • 7 •
## Last Laughs
277

## Introduction

We know that no kid ever reads
an introduction.
So we're just going to skip it.

**1**

LET'S MAKE A DILL!

SPECIAL
ALL
RIDDLES
DRASTICALLY
REDUCED!

*Jokes and Riddles*

Q: Who is beautiful, gray, and wears glass slippers?
A: Cinderelephant.

Q: What is gray, weighs two tons, and has wings?
A: Cinderelephant's fairy godmother.

JACK: What did the elephant rock 'n' roll star say into the microphone?
JILL: I don't know. What?
JACK: "Tusking—one, two, three. Tusking—one, two, three."

MACK: I can lift an elephant with one hand.
MOE: I don't believe you.
MACK: Get me an elephant with one hand and I'll show you.

SAL: What is the difference between an elephant and a mattababy?
SUE: What's a mattababy?
SAL: Why, nothing. What's the matter with you?

BOB: Why do elephants paint their toenails red?
BETTY: I don't know. Why?
BOB: So they can hide in the strawberry patch.
BETTY: I don't believe that.
BOB: Did you ever see an elephant in a strawberry patch?
BETTY: No!
BOB: See? It works!

Q: When is an elephant like a cute little bunny rabbit?
A: When he's wearing his cute little bunny rabbit suit.

TEACHER: Frankie, can you define "nonsense"?
FRANKIE: An elephant hanging over a cliff with his tail wrapped around a daisy.

Q: What time is it when a elephant sits on a park bench?
A: Time to get a new bench.

Q: Why did the elephant sit on the marshmallow?
A: To keep from falling into the cocoa.

Q: What do you do with old bowling balls?
A: Give them to elephants to use as marbles.

Q: How can you tell when there's an elephant in the refrigerator?
A: You can't close the door.

Q: How do you run over an elephant?
A: Climb up its tail, dash to its head, and slide down its trunk.

Q: What do you get when you cross an elephant with a computer?
Q: A ten-thousand-pound know-it-all.

Q: If you saw nine elephants walking down the street with red socks and one elephant walking down the street with green socks, what would this prove?
A: That nine out of ten elephants wear red socks.

Q: How do you make an elephant stew?
A: Keep it waiting for two hours.

Q: What do you get if you cross an elephant with a canary?
A: A pretty messy cage.

Q: What do you find between elephants' toes?
A: Slow-running people.

Q: How do you stop an elephant from charging?
A: Take away his credit cards.

Q: How do you make an elephant float?
A: Put two scoops of ice cream, some milk, and soda water in a glass. Add one elephant.

Q: How do you get five elephants into a Volkswagen?
A: Put two in front, two in back, and one in the glove compartment.

Q: How can you tell when there's an elephant in the back seat of your car?
A: You can smell the peanuts on its breath.

Q: What's the difference between an elephant and a grape?
A: The grape is purple.

Q: What did the Lone Ranger say when he saw his horse coming?

A: "Here comes my horse."

Q: What did Tarzan say when he saw a herd of elephants coming?

A: "Here come the elephants."

Q: What did Jane say when she saw the herd of elephants coming?

A: "Here come the grapes." (She was color-blind.)

Q: Who started all these elephant jokes?

A: That's what the elephants want to know.

Q: How can you tell an elephant from a grape?

A: Jump up and down on it for a while. If you don't get any wine, it's an elephant.

Q: What do you call a hamburger bun in a rocking chair?
A: Rockin' roll.

Q: What TV show do pickles like best?
A: "Let's Make a Dill."

Q: What's green, noisy, and very dangerous?
A: A herd of stampeding pickles.

Q: What do cowboys put on their pancakes?
A: Maple stirrup.

Q: What do you call a banana that has been stepped on?
A: A banana splat.

WAITER: How did you find your steak, sir?
DINER: I lifted up the mushroom and there it was.

HE: Would you join me in a cup of tea?
SHE: You get in first.

MAN IN SNACK BAR: I would like a glass of milk and a
    muttered buffin.
WAITER: You mean a buffered muttin, don't you?
MAN: No, I mean a muffered buttin.
WAITER: Wouldn't you rather just have some toast?

Q: What do you have if you cross two ducks and a cow?
A: Quackers and milk.

CUSTOMER: What's the difference between the blue-plate
    and the white-plate specials?
WAITER: The white-plate special is ten cents extra.
CUSTOMER: Is the food any better?
WAITER: No, but we wash the plate.

Q: What's yellow and wears a mask?
A: The Lone Lemon.

Q: If a butcher is six feet tall
    and wears a size twelve shoe,
        what does he weigh?
A: Meat, of course.

Q: What's the best thing to put into a pie?
A: Your teeth.

DINER: Is there any soup on the menu?
WAITER: There was, but I wiped it off.

Q: What do you get when you cross a chicken with a dog?
A: Pooched eggs.

Q: What do you call a fish with two knees?
A: A two-knee fish.

Q: What did the mayonnaise say to the refrigerator?
A: "Close the door. I'm dressing."

The restaurant sign said, "We Fought the Roaches," so the man went in and ordered soup.
MAN: Waiter, why is there a roach in my soup? The sign said you fought the roaches.
WAITER: It didn't say we won.

Q: What do you get when you cross a frog and a potato?
A: A potatoad.

Q: What does a shark eat with peanut butter?
A: Jellyfish.

Q: Name five things that contain milk.
A: Butter, cheese, ice cream, and two cows.

FUSSY CUSTOMER: Just look at this chicken you served me. One leg is longer than the other.
WAITER: Were you planning to eat it or dance with it?

DINER: Waiter, I still didn't get the turtle soup I ordered.
WAITER: Sorry, but you know how slow turtles are.

CUSTOMER: I'd like a hamburger. Will it be long?
WAITER: No. It will be round, as usual.

Two astronauts opened the first restaurant on the moon. The food was good, but the restaurant lacked atmosphere.

DINER: Waiter, do you serve crabs here?
WAITER: Sit down. We serve anybody.

CUSTOMER: This soup isn't fit for a pig!
WAITER: Then I will bring you some that is!

WAITER: Shall I cut your pizza into six or twelve pieces?
CUSTOMER: Only six, please. I couldn't possibly eat twelve
pieces.

WAITER: Have you tried the meatballs, sir?
CUSTOMER: Yes—and I found them guilty.

CUSTOMER: What is this fly doing in my soup?
WAITER: Looks like the backstroke to me.

CUSTOMER: Waiter, there's a fly drowning in my soup!
WAITER: Quick, give him mouth-to-mouth resuscitation!

CUSTOMER: Waiter, there's a fly in my black bean soup!
WAITER: Very well, madam. I'll take it to the chef and he'll
exchange it for a bean.

CUSTOMER: Waiter, there's a fly in my soup.
WAITER: Don't worry about it. He won't eat too much.

CUSTOMER: Waiter, there's a dead fly in my soup!
WAITER: It's the heat that kills them, sir.

CUSTOMER: What is this fly doing in my ice cream?
WAITER: He must like winter sports.

TEACHER: If you stood with your back to the north and faced due south, what would be on your left hand?
DEBBIE: Fingers.

TEACHER: If you add 500, 391, 38, 162, and 17, then divide by 39, what would you get?
STUART: The wrong answer.

TEACHER: Oscar, if you had five pieces of candy and Joey asked you for one, how many pieces would you have left?
OSCAR: Five.

TEACHER: How did you get that horrible swelling on your nose?
SMART SCOTT: I bent over to smell a brose.
TEACHER: There's no *b* in rose.
SMART SCOTT: There was in this one.

TEACHER: Yes, what is it?

FAILING STUDENT: I don't want to frighten you, but Dad said that if I don't get better grades, someone's going to get a spanking.

TEACHER: Suzie, please spell "cattle."

SUZIE: C–A–T–T–T–L–E.

TEACHER: Leave out one of the *t*'s.

SUZIE: Which one?

TEACHER: It's the law of gravity that keeps us from falling off the earth.

SILLY SALLY: What kept us from falling off before the law was passed?

ARNIE: I wish I had been born a thousand years ago.

LES: Why?

ARNIE: Just think of all the history I wouldn't have to study.

TEACHER: Donald, I hope I didn't see you looking at Annie's paper.

DONALD: I hope you didn't either!

TEACHER: Birds, though small, are remarkable creatures. For example, what can a bird do that I can't do?

EAGER EARL: Take a bath in a saucer.

TEACHER: Why are you crawling into class, Arthur?
ARTHUR: Because class has already started and you said, "Don't anyone dare walk into my class late!"

TEACHER: When you think of Greece, what's the first thing that comes to your mind?
STUDENT: French fries.

Q: Where was the Declaration of Independence signed?
A: At the bottom.

TEACHER: Harvey, you didn't wash your face this morning, did you? I can see you had eggs for breakfast.
HARVEY: No, I didn't, teacher. I had cereal. I had eggs yesterday!

JERRY: I'm not going to school today, Mom. Nobody there likes me.

MOTHER: That's nonsense, Jerry. Besides, you have to go to school today. You're the principal.


BILLY'S MOTHER: Billy told me he got 100 on his tests yesterday!

BILLY'S TEACHER: He did—50 in spelling and 50 in arithmetic.


TEACHER: Jack, how do you spell "Mississippi"?

JACK: The river or the state?


Q: Do you know Lincoln's Gettysburg Address?

A: I thought he lived in the White House.


SCIENCE TEACHER: Now, this is a dogwood tree.

STUDENT: How can you tell?

SCIENCE TEACHER: Because of its bark.


TEACHER: Which is more important, the sun or the moon?

STUDENT: The moon.

TEACHER: Why do you say that?

STUDENT: The moon shines at night when it's dark, but the sun shines in the day when it's light anyway.


TEACHER: Jerry, give me the formula for water.

JERRY: H, I, J, K, L, M, N, O.

TEACHER: What kind of a crazy answer is that?

JERRY: You told us that water was H to O.

TEACHER: Name the four seasons.
STUDENT: Salt, pepper, sugar, and spice.

STUDENT: I don't think I deserve a zero on this test.
TEACHER: Neither do I. But it's the lowest grade I can give
    you.

FATHER: Why is your January report card marked so low?
SON: Well, you know how it is, Dad. After Christmas
    everything is marked down.

"Say, Mom," said Steve. "There's a special PTA meet-
ing at school this afternoon."

"Really?" said his mother. "What's so special about
it?"

"It's just for you," said Steve. "Oh yes, the principal,
my teacher, and I have been invited, too."

The boy came home from school with a zero on his
paper.

"Why did you get the zero?" his mother asked.

"That's no zero," the boy answered.

"Teacher ran out of stars,
  so she gave me the moon."

MATH TEACHER: And so we find that X equals zero.
STUDENT: Gee. All that work for nothing.

TEACHER: You can't sleep in my class!
STUDENT: I could if you didn't talk so loudly.

TEACHER: Frank, if you found three dollars in your right
pocket and two dollars in your left pocket, what
would you have?
FRANK: Somebody else's pants on.

JACK: Hooray! The teacher said we would have a test—
rain or shine.
JOAN: But that's nothing to be happy about.
JACK: It's snowing.

TEACHER: If I lay one egg on this chair and two on the
table, how many will I have altogether?
SYLVESTER: Personally, I don't believe you can do it.

DAUGHTER: Dad, can you write your name in the dark?
DAD: I think so.
DAUGHTER: Great. Would you please turn off the lights and sign my report card?

A boy wrote this letter from boarding school:
Dear Mom and Dad:
  Gue$$ what I need? Plea$e $end $ome $oon.
    Be$t Wi$he$,
      Your $on, $ammy
The parents' reply:
Dear Sammy:
  NOthing much is happening here. Please write aNOther letter soon. Bye for NOw.
    Love,
      Dad and Mom

VOICE ON THE PHONE: Is this the principal?
PRINCIPAL: Yes.
VOICE ON THE PHONE: Jenny Smith is too sick to come to school today.
PRINCIPAL: Who's calling, please?
VOICE ON THE PHONE: This is my mother.

Q: Where do sheep get their hair cut?
A: At the baa-baa shop.

Q: Why did they fire the goose from the basketball team?
A: Too many fowl plays.

Q: Who saw the Brontosaurus enter the restaurant?
A: The diners saw.

Q: What happened to the cat who swallowed a flash-
light?
A: He hiccuped with delight.

Q: Why is it hard to talk with a goat around?
A: Because he keeps butting in.

Q: On the way to the water hole, a zebra met four elephants. Each elephant had three monkeys on its
back. Each monkey had two birds on its tail. How
many animals in all were going to the water hole?
A: Only one. The rest were coming back from the water
hole.

Q: What dog says "meow"?
A: A police dog working undercover.

Q: What kind of key won't open a door?
A: A monkey.

Q: Why does a mother kangaroo hope it doesn't rain?
A: She hates it when the children have to stay inside.

Q: What do you call a sleeping bull?
A: A bulldozer.

ANN: Did you hear about the cat who swallowed a ball of
     yarn?
AL: No, tell me.
ANN: She had mittens.

Q: Where do otters come from?
A: Otter space.

Q: Why did the fly fly?
A: The spider spied her.

Q: Why did they let a turkey join the band?
A: He had the drumsticks.

Q: Why do cows wear bells?
A: Their horns don't work.

Q: Why did the chicken cross the road?
A: The light was green.

Q: Why did the chicken want to get to the other side?
A: It wanted to see a man lay bricks.

Q: Why did the duck cross the road?
A: The chicken was on vacation.

ANN: My dog is a baseball dog.
STAN: What makes him a baseball dog?
ANN: He catches flies, chases fowls, and beats it for home
     when he sees the catcher coming.

Q: Why don't ducks tell jokes while they are flying?
A: Because they would quack up.

Q: Why do bees hum?
A: They don't know the words.

Q: How do you communicate with a fish?
A: Drop him a line.

Q: Why does a monkey scratch himself?
A: He's the only one who knows where it itches.

Q: Why should you not tell pigs secrets?
A: Because pigs are squealers.

Q: Why do chickens get their mouths washed out with soap?
A: Because they use fowl language.

Q: What did the baby porcupine say when he backed
   into a cactus?
A: "Is that you, Mama?"

Q: How would you start a lightning bug race?
A: On your mark, get set, glow!

Q: What animal never plays fair?
A: The cheetah.

Q: What's the best way to keep a skunk from smelling?
A: Hold its nose.

Q: What happens to a cat who eats a lemon?
A: It turns into a sourpuss.

Q: Why did Snoopy quit?
A: He was tired of working for Peanuts.

Q: Who performs operations at the fish hospital?
A: The head sturgeon.

Q: What is smarter than a talking horse?
A: A spelling bee.

Q: What do you call a rabbit with fleas?
A: Bugs Bunny.

Q: What do you call two spiders who just got married?
A: Newlywebs.

Q: What is green, has six legs, and can jump over your head?
A: A grasshopper with the hiccups.


Q: Where do cows go on dates?
A: To the moo-vies.

LITTLE WORM: Am I late, Mother?
MOTHER WORM: Yes, where in earth have you been?


BOY: I'd like a quarter's worth of birdseed, please.
STOREKEEPER: How many birds do you have?
BOY: None, but I want to grow some.


Q: What goes 999-*thump*, 999-*thump*, 999-*thump?*
A: A centipede with a wooden leg.


Q: What has four legs and goes "Oom! Oom!"?
A: A cow walking backward.

Q: What's the best way to catch a rabbit?
A: Hide behind a bush and make a noise like a carrot.

Q: What has four legs and flies?
A: A horse in the summertime.

Q: How does a hippopotamus get up a tree?
A: Climbs on an acorn and waits.

Q: How does a hippopotamus get down from a tree?
A: He sits on a leaf and waits for the fall.

KNOCK KNOCK JOKES!

Knock, knock.
  Who's there?
Pencil.
  Pencil who?
Pencil fall down if
  you don't wear a belt.

Knock, knock.
  Who's there?
Tuscaloosa.
  Tuscaloosa who?
Tuscaloosa on
  older elephants.

Knock, knock.
  Who's there?
Diesel.
  Diesel who?
Diesel make you laugh
  if you're not too smart.

Knock, knock.
  Who's there?
Boo.
  Boo who?
Don't cry.
  It's only a joke!

Knock, knock.
  Who's there?
Turnip.
  Turnip who?
Turnip your pants—
  they're too long.

Knock, knock.
  Who's there?
Banana.
  Banana who?
Knock, knock.
  Who's there?
Banana.
  Banana who?
Knock, knock.
  Who's there?
Orange.
  Orange who?
Orange you glad I didn't say banana?

Knock, knock.
  Who's there?
Mandy.
  Mandy who?
Mandy lifeboats!

Knock, knock.
  Who's there?
Tuba.
  Tuba who?
Tuba toothpaste.

Knock, knock.
  Who's there?
Fire engine.
  Fire engine who?
Fire engine one and prepare for blast-off!

Knock, knock.
  Who's there?
Lettuce.
  Lettuce who?
Lettuce in. It's cold out here.

Knock, knock.
  Who's there?
Philip.
  Philip who?
Philip the tub. I want to take a bath.

Knock, knock.
   Who's there?
Amos.
   Amos who?
Amos-quito just bit me!

Knock, knock.
   Who's there?
Abby.
   Abby who?
Abby birthday to you.

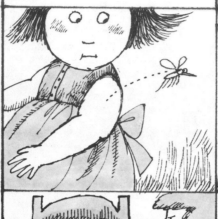

Knock, knock.
   Who's there?
Dewey.
   Dewey who?
Dewey have to go
   to school today?

Knock, knock.
   Who's there?
Daniel.
   Daniel who?
Daniel so loud!
   I can hear you.

Knock, knock.
  Who's there?
Rita.
  Rita who?
Rita good book lately?

Knock, knock.
  Who's there?
Ringo.
  Ringo who?
Ringo round the collar.

Knock, knock.
  Who's there?
Juan.
  Juan who?
Juan, two, three, four!
  When you gonna open
the door?

Knock, knock.
  Who's there?
Rocky.
  Rocky who?
Rocky-bye baby in
  the treetop.

Knock, knock.
Who's there?
Tim.
Tim who?
Tim-ber!!

Knock, knock.
Who's there?
Little old lady.
Little old lady who?
I didn't know
you could yodel.

Knock, knock.
Who's there?
Wooden.
Wooden who?
Wooden you
like to know.

Knock, knock.
Who's there?
Hammond.
Hammond who?
Hammond eggs
is good for breakfast.

Knock, knock.
Who's there?
Farm.
Farm who?
Farm-e to know and
you to find out.

Knock, knock.
Who's there?
Hoo.
Hoo who?
What are you, an owl?

Knock, knock.
Who's there?
Russell.
Russell who?
Russell me up
something to eat.

Knock, knock.
Who's there?
Dishes.
Dishes who?
Dishes your mother!
Now open the door!

Knock, knock.
Who's there?
Hatch.
Hatch who?
Gesundheit!

Knock, knock.
Who's there?
Police.
Police who?
Police open up.
I forgot
my lunch.

DOCTOR: What's the matter with your wife?
HUSBAND: She thinks she's a chicken.
DOCTOR: That's terrible. How long has she been this way?
HUSBAND: For three years.
DOCTOR: Why didn't you bring her to see me sooner?
HUSBAND: We needed the eggs.


PATIENT: My foot falls asleep and wakes me up.
DOCTOR: If your foot is asleep, how can it wake you up?
PATIENT: It snores.


LOU: I think I'm sick. Call me a doctor.
SUE: Okay. You're a doctor.

PATIENT: My stomach's been aching ever since I ate those twelve oysters yesterday.

DOCTOR: Were they fresh?

PATIENT: I don't know.

DOCTOR: Well, how did they look when you opened the shells?

PATIENT: You're supposed to open the shells?


PATIENT: I was just bitten on the leg by a dog.

DOCTOR: Did you put anything on it?

PATIENT: No. He liked it just the way it was.

BOY: Did you hear about the new doctor doll?

GIRL: No. What's it like?

BOY: You wind it up and it operates on batteries.


PATIENT: Doctor, you must help me. I can't remember anything.

DOCTOR: How long has this been going on?

PATIENT: How long has *what* been going on?


PATIENT: I am not well, Doctor.

DOCTOR: What seems to be the trouble?

PATIENT: I work like a horse, eat like a bird, and I'm as tired as a dog.

DOCTOR: Sounds to me like you ought to see a veterinarian.

PATIENT: Doctor, you have to help me. I snore so loud I wake myself up.
DOCTOR: Then you'll have to sleep in another room.

PATIENT: Doctor, I think corn is growing out of my ears.
DOCTOR: Why, so it is. How did this happen?
PATIENT: Beats me. I planted radishes.

PATIENT: Oh! Ouch! Oh! Ouch!
DOCTOR: Stop yelling. I haven't put the needle in yet.
PATIENT: I know. But you're standing on my foot.

PATIENT: Doctor, that ointment you gave me makes my arm smart.
DOCTOR: In that case, rub some on your head.

DOCTOR: I'm afraid you have canary disease.
PATIENT: Can you cure me, Doc?
DOCTOR: Yes, it's tweetable.

MACK: I just had my appendix removed.
MOE: Have a scar?
MACK: No, thanks. I don't smoke.

PATIENT: Doc, after the operation on my hands, will I be
    able to play the piano?
DOCTOR: Of course.
PATIENT: That's wonderful. I've never been able to play
    the piano before.

"Doctor," asked the patient anxiously, "if I let you
operate on me, can you promise that I'll be back playing
the piano in a week or two?"

"Well, I can't promise the piano," replied the doctor
cheerfully, "but the last patient I operated on was playing a harp within twenty-four hours."

DOCTOR: Have you been taking care of your cold?
PATIENT: I've had it for weeks now and it seems good as new.

PATIENT: I feel funny, Doctor. What should I do?
DOCTOR: Go on television.

PATIENT *(on telephone):* Doctor, I have the strangest symptoms. My head feels squeezed, I smell something peculiar, my voice sounds strange, and one foot is cold. What could be the matter?
DOCTOR: You probably have a sock pulled over your head.

PATIENT: I just swallowed my harmonica. What should I
do?
DOCTOR: Be happy.
PATIENT: Be happy about what?
DOCTOR: Be happy you weren't playing the piano.


DOCTOR: Stick out your tongue.
PATIENT: What for? I'm not mad at you.

PATIENT: Doctor, last night I dreamed I ate a giant marsh-
mallow.
DOCTOR: What's so bad about that?
PATIENT: When I woke up, the pillow was gone.

MRS. JONES: Doctor, my husband thinks he's a parking meter.

PSYCHIATRIST: That's serious. Have him come to see me this Friday.

MRS. JONES: I'm sorry, he can't make it. Friday is the day they come and take the coins out of his mouth.

PSYCHIATRIST: Mr. Johnson, I think you're suffering from a split personality.
MR. JOHNSON: No, we aren't.

PATIENT: Doctor, I have this terrible problem when I go shopping. I take home everything that's marked down.
PSYCHIATRIST: Why is that such a problem?
PATIENT: Last week I took home an escalator.

PSYCHIATRIST: What do you dream about at night?
PATIENT: Baseball.
DOCTOR: Don't you dream about anything else?
PATIENT: What—and miss my turn at bat?

"There's nothing wrong with you," said the psychiatrist to his patient. "Why, you're as sane as I am."

"But, Doctor!" said the patient as he brushed wildly at himself. "It's the butterflies! They're all over me!"

"For heaven's sake," cried the doctor. "Don't brush them off on me!"

Psychiatrists tell us that one out of four people is mentally ill. So check your friends—if three of them seem to be all right, you're the one.

DOCTOR: Did you take the patient's temperature?
NURSE: No, is it missing?


DOCTOR: What is the condition of the boy who swallowed
    the quarter?
NURSE: No change yet.

# Dentist Jokes

DENTIST: Good grief. You have the biggest cavity I've ever
seen . . . ever seen . . . ever seen.
PATIENT: You don't have to repeat yourself.
DENTIST: I didn't. That was an echo.

# Veterinarian Jokes

DOG OWNER: I'm worried, Doc. I think my dog has ticks.
What should I do?
VETERINARIAN: Don't wind him.

Q: What do you call an operation on a rabbit?
A: A hare-cut.

EYE DOCTOR: Is there any letter on the chart that you can't read?
PATIENT: What chart?

Q: What kind of dances do opticians go to?
A: Eye balls.

PATIENT: Doctor, I've been seeing fuzzy spots in front of my eyes. Can you give me glasses?
OPTOMETRIST: Why, yes. How are these?
PATIENT: Great. I see the spots much more clearly now.

OPTOMETRIST: Have your eyes been checked lately?
PATIENT: No, they've always been plain brown.

# Spooky Jokes

Q: What kind of horses go out after dark?
A: Night mares.

SECRETARY: The Invisible Man is at the door.
BOSS: Tell him I can't see him.

Q: How do witches tell time?
A: By a witch watch, of course.

Q: What did the father ghost tell the little ghost?
A: "Don't spook until you're spooken to."

Q: What do you get when you cross peanut butter, bread, jelly, and a werewolf?
A: A peanut butter and jelly sandwich that howls and gets hairy when the full moon rises.

Q: Why was the witch first in her class?
A: She was the best speller.

Q: What was the first place Dracula visited when he went
to New York?
A: The Vampire State Building.
Q: Why didn't they want him hanging around?
A: Because he was a pain in the neck.

CHILD: Mommy, all the kids say I look like a werewolf.
MOTHER: Shut up and comb your face.

Q: Why does the Frankenstein monster look so stiff when
he walks?
A: Because Mrs. Frankenstein put too much starch in his
underwear.

Q: What do sea monsters eat?
A: Fish and ships.

Q: What is a ghost's favorite food?
A: Spook-ghetti.

Q: How do you greet a three-headed monster?
A: "Hello. Hello. Hello. How are you? How are you?
How are you?"

Q: What is a monster's normal eyesight?
A: 20-20-20-20-20.

Q: What was the vampire doing on the highway?
A: Looking for the main artery.

MONSTER ONE: That girl over there rolled her eyes at me. What should I do?
MONSTER TWO: If you are a real gentleman, you will pick them up and roll them back to her.

MONSTER ONE: Did you hear about Freddy? He died when he drank a gallon of varnish.
MONSTER TWO: That's too bad.
MONSTER ONE: Yes, but they say he had a lovely finish.

Q: What did the witch's broom say to her baby?
A: "Go to sweep, little baby."

Q: What do you call a skeleton that pushes your door-bell?
A: A dead ringer.

BABY: Mommy, what's a vampire?
MOTHER: Don't ask silly questions. Drink your tomato juice before it clots.

Q: What do you get if you cross a monster with a parrot?
A: I don't know, but you give it a cracker when it asks for one.

The vampire took an ocean cruise. He went into the dining room and said, "I'm starving."

"Would you like to see a menu?" asked the waiter.

"No, just show me the passenger list," answered the vampire.

Q: What do you call a skeleton that won't get out of bed?
A: Lazy bones.

Q: What do witches eat for dinner?
A: Halloweenies.

FIRST ASTRONAUT: What has 6 eyes, 10 arms, and is green all over?

SECOND ASTRONAUT: I don't know.

FIRST ASTRONAUT: I don't know either, but it's looking in our window.

TIM: Why do monsters have square shoulders?
JIM: Because they eat lots of cereal.
TIM: How can cereal give them square shoulders?
JIM: It's not the cereal. It's the boxes!

MONSTER MOTHER TO CHILD: I told you never to speak with someone in your mouth!

Q: Do vampires have holidays?
A: Sure. Haven't you ever heard of Fangsgiving Day?

FIRST MONSTER *(after catching an airplane in flight):* How do you eat one of these things?
SECOND MONSTER: Like a peanut. Just break it open and eat what's inside!

CHILD MONSTER: Mother, I hate my teacher.
MOTHER MONSTER: Then just eat your salad.

Q: Why didn't the skeleton have a good time at the prom?
A: He had no body to dance with.

Dr. Frankenstein sent Igor to get two fresh bodies. Igor went to the cemetery and dug up two bodies from a grave marked "John and Grace Hill." While Dr. Frankenstein worked on the bodies, he asked Igor to play some music on the radio. As soon as the music started, the two bodies came to life and got up from the table.

Igor said, "The Hills are alive with the sound of music."

Dracula was lying in his coffin sleeping one bright, sunny day. For a prank, some boys nailed roller skates to the coffin and sent it rolling down a hill. It narrowly missed people and cars and went crashing through a drugstore window. As the coffin sped through the drugstore, the startled pharmacist heard Dracula say, "You got anything to help stop this coffin?"

# PUN FUN

Q: What did the big firecracker say to the little firecracker?
A: "My pop's bigger than your pop."

BEN: How much is five Q and five Q?
Ten Q.
BILL: You're welcome.
BEN:

Two racehorses met in a paddock. One said to the other, "I can't remember your name, but your pace is familiar."

LETTER RIDDLES

Q: What two letters describe a slippery sidewalk?
A: IC.

Q: What letters contain nothing?
A: MT.

Q: What is at the end of everything?
A: The letter *g*.

Q: What letter is an insect?
A: B.

Q: What letter is part of your head?
A: I.

"I love hot dogs," Tom said frankly.

"These jeans are too tight," Tom panted.

"Let's go to the rodeo," Tom said hoarsely.

"I'm raising a billy goat," Tom said gruffly.

"Can't you keep that dog quiet?" Tom barked.

"I brought you these candies," Tom said sweetly.

"I hear an owl," Tom hooted.

"Is this sweater 100 percent wool?" asked Tom sheepishly.

Q: Why doesn't a bike stand up by itself?
A: It's two-tired.

Q: Why is 6 afraid of 7?
A: Because 7 8 9!

Q: What did the rug say to the floor?
A: "Stay where you are. I've got you covered."

Q: What did the judge say when a skunk walked into the court room?
A: "Odor in the court!"

Q: Can a person have a nose
twelve inches long?
A: No. Then it would be a foot.

GIRL: Where does the Lone Ranger take his garbage?
BOY: To the dump, to the dump, to the dump, dump,
dump.

JAKE: Where did King Richard III keep his armies?
JACK: Up his sleevies.

Q: What's purple and conquered the world?
A: Alexander the Grape.

Q: What's the happiest state in the Union?
A: Merry-land. (Maryland.)

Q: How do you send a message in the forest?
A: By moss code.

Q: What's white and flies up?
A: A confused snowflake.

DAN: What's purple and green with yellow and black
stripes and has a hundred legs?
DONNA: I don't know.
DAN: I don't know either, but it's crawling up your neck.

Q: What did one tonsil say to the other?
A: "Get dressed. The doctor's taking us out tonight."

Q: What did one flea say to the other when they came out of the theater?
A: "Shall we walk or take a dog?"

Q: What's white and black with a cherry on top?
A: A police car.

Q: What did the robot say to the gas pump?
A: "Take your finger out of your ear."

Q: How long is the song "Soap, Soap, Soap, Soap, Soap"?
A: About five bars.

Q: Why did the traffic light turn red?
A: So would you if you had to change in the middle of the street.

Q: Why did Humpty Dumpty have a great fall?
A: He wanted to make up for a bad summer.

Q: Why did the burglar take a bath?
A: He wanted to make a clean getaway.

Q: Why is tennis such a noisy game?
A: Because each player raises a racquet.

Q: When is a bike not a bike?
A: When it turns into a driveway.

Q: What can speak every language in the world?
A: An echo.

PASSENGER: Is this my train?
CONDUCTOR: No, it belongs to the train company.

PASSENGER: Can I take this train to New York?
CONDUCTOR: No, it's much too heavy.

Q: If Miss-issippi should lend Miss-ouri her New Jersey,
    what would Dela-ware?
A: I don't know. Al-aska.

Q: What lies at the bottom of the sea and shakes?
A: A nervous wreck.

A man went to the rocket station and asked for a
ticket to the moon.

"Sorry, sir," the attendant said, "the moon is full just
now."

Q: What did Cinderella say to the photographer?
A: "Someday my prints will come."

Q: Did you hear about the robbery at the laundromat?
A: Two clothespins held up a shirt.

Q: What did the beach say as the tide came in?
A: "Long time, no sea."

Q: What is the biggest jewel in the world?
A: A baseball diamond.

Q: What has hands but never washes its face?
A: A clock.

Q: What did one elevator say to the other?
A: "I think I'm coming down with something."

Q: What did one potato chip say to the other?
A: "Let's go for a dip."

SAM: Three large men were standing under one small umbrella. There was thunder and lightning. But no one got wet.

SANDY: Why?

SAM: It wasn't raining.

Shy Shelly says she shall sew sheets.

Unique New York.

Three free throws.

Sam's shop stocks short spotted socks.

Knapsack straps.

Lesser leather never weathered wetter weather better.

Inchworms itching.

The myth of Miss Muffet.

Friendly Frank flips fine flapjacks.

Lovely lemon liniment.

Fat frogs flying past fast.

A tooter who tooted a flute
   Tried to tutor two tutors to toot.
Said the two to their tutor,
   "Is it harder to toot or
To tutor two tutors to toot?"

Here's to you two and to we two too;
  If you love we two
    As we love you two,
    Then here's to we four:
But if you don't love we two
  As we two love you two,
  Then here's to we two
  And no more.

Flee from fog to fight flu fast!

Greek grapes.

Thieves seize skis.

Mr. See owned a saw.
  And Mr. Soar owned a seesaw.
Now See's saw sawed Soar's seesaw
  Before Soar saw See,
Which made Soar sore.
  Had Soar seen See's saw
Before See sawed Soar's seesaw,
  See's saw would not have sawed
Soar's seesaw.
  So See's saw sawed Soar's seesaw.
But it was sad to see Soar so sore
  Just because See's saw sawed
Soar's seesaw!

We surely shall see the sun shine soon.

Moose noshing much mush.

Sly Sam slurps Sally's soup.

Six short slow shepherds.

Peter Piper picked a peck of pickled peppers.
If Peter Piper picked a peck of pickled peppers,
Where's the peck of pickled peppers Peter Piper
picked?

Sally sells seashells by the seashore.
Surely she will sell some seashells soon.

Which witch wished which wicked wish?

The two-twenty-two train tore through the tunnel.

How much wood would a woodchuck chuck
If a woodchuck could chuck wood?
A woodchuck would chuck all the wood he could
chuck,
If a woodchuck could chuck wood.

Three gray geese in the green grass grazing.
Gray were the geese and green was the grass.

Many an anemone sees an enemy anemone.

A tree toad loved a she-toad
  Who lived up in a tree.
He was a two-toed tree toad
  But a three-toed toad was she.
The two-toed tree toad tried to win
  The three-toed she-toad's heart,
For the two-toed tree toad loved the ground
  That the three-toed tree toad trod.
But the two-toed tree toad tried in vain.
  He couldn't please her whim.
From her tree toad bower
  With her three-toed power
The she-toad vetoed him.

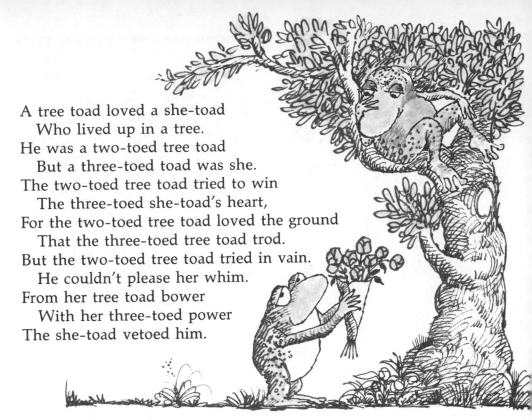

Quick—Quack—Quock
Quack—Quock—Quick
Quock—Quick—Quack


Say this sharply, say this sweetly,
Say this shortly, say this softly.
Say this sixteen times in succession.


I often sit and think
and fish and sit
and fish and think
and sit and fish
and think and wish
that I could get a cool drink!

Nine nice night nurses nursing nicely.

Peggy Babcock.

A flea and a fly flew up in a flue.
Said the flea, "Let us fly!"
Said the fly, "Let us flee!"
So they flew through a flaw in the flue.

Black bug's blood.

Flash message!

Six sticky sucker sticks.

Six sharp smart sharks.

If Stu chews shoes, should Stu
choose the shoes he chews?

Crisp crusts crackle crunchily.

Sure the ship's shipshape, sir.

Double Bubble gum bubbles double.

Betty better butter Brad's bread.

If one doctor doctors another doctor, does the doctor
who doctors the doctor doctor the doctor the way the
doctor he is doctoring doctors? Or does he doctor
the doctor the way the doctor who doctors doctors?

Betty Botter bought some butter.
"But," she said, "the butter's bitter.
If I put it in my batter,
It will make my batter bitter.
But a bit of better butter—
*That* would make my batter better."
So she bought a bit of butter,
Better than her bitter butter.
And she put it in her batter,
And the batter was not bitter.
So 'twas better Betty Botter
Bought a bit of better butter.

You've no need to light a night-light
On a light night like tonight,
For a night-light's light's a slight light,
And tonight's a night that's light.
When a night's light, like tonight's light,
It is really not quite right
To light night-lights with their slight lights
On a light night like tonight.

Brad's big black bath brush broke.

Sixish.

A batch of mixed biscuits.

I thought a thought.
But the thought I thought wasn't the thought
I thought I thought.
Or was it?

Six shimmering sharks sharply striking shins.

A swim well swum is a well swum swim.
So swim, swan, swim.

Three little ghosteses
Sitting on posteses
Eating buttered toasteses,
Smeared up with greaseses
Running down their cheekseses
Down to their kneeseses,
Nasty little beasteses!

# 3
# IS YOUR REFRIGERATOR RUNNING?

*Tricks,*

*Games,*

*and Puzzles*

YOU: I was on TV yesterday.

FRIEND: You were?!

YOU: Yes, but my mother made me get off. She was afraid I would break it.

YOU SAY: Adam and Eve and Pinch-Me
Went down to the river to bathe.
Adam and Eve were drowned.
Which of the three was saved?

YOUR FRIEND SAYS: Pinch-Me.

*(You pinch him.)*

YOU SAY: What's your name?
YOUR FRIEND SAYS: Mary (or John, or whatever).
YOU: What's this? *(Point to your nose.)*
FRIEND: Nose.
YOU: What's in my hand? *(Show an empty hand.)*
FRIEND: Nothing.
YOU: You said it. "Mary knows *(nose)* nothing!"

YOU: After everything I say, you say, "Just like me,"
    okay?
FRIEND: Okay.
YOU: I went into a haunted house.
FRIEND: Just like me.
YOU: I went up the stairs.
FRIEND: Just like me.
YOU: I went into a room.
FRIEND: Just like me.
YOU: I saw a bed.
FRIEND: Just like me.
YOU: In the bed was a monkey.
FRIEND: Just like me.

YOU: I bet I can make you say "purple."
FRIEND: I bet you can't.
YOU: What colors are in the American flag?
FRIEND: Red, white, and blue.
YOU: I told you I could make you say "blue."
FRIEND: No, you didn't.
YOU: I didn't?
FRIEND: No, you said "purple."
YOU: See? You just said it.

YOU: I say, "I one a garbage can." And you say, "I two a
    garbage can" and so on. Okay?
FRIEND: Okay.
YOU: I one a garbage can.
FRIEND: I two a garbage can.
YOU: I three a garbage can.
FRIEND: I four a garbage can.
YOU: I five a garbage can.
FRIEND: I six a garbage can.
YOU: I seven a garbage can.
FRIEND: I eight a garbage can.
YOU: You *ate* a garbage can? Ugh!

YOU: In the Everglades, there are birds that sit on branches and bark. True or false?

FRIEND: False. I don't believe it.

YOU: It's true. The branches they sit on have bark, don't they?

YOU: Is your refrigerator running?

FRIEND: Yes.

YOU: Better go catch it.

YOU: What do you have on under there?

FRIEND: Under where?

YOU: That's right! *(underwear)*

FRIEND: Did you get a haircut?

YOU: Sure, I got them all cut.

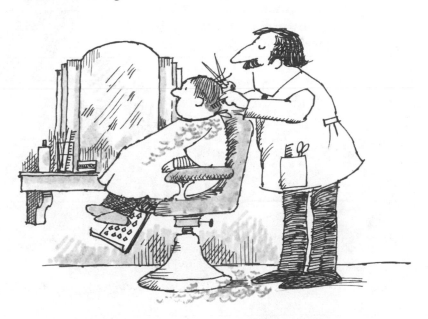

YOU: If a rooster on a farm in Connecticut ran across the state line and laid an egg on a railroad track in New York, who owns the egg: the state of New York, the farmer, or the railroad?

FRIEND: I don't know.

YOU: No one. Roosters don't lay eggs.

YOU: Can you solve a problem for me?

FRIEND: I'll try.

YOU: You take one bushel of sawdust, two bales of hay, and two hundred cotton balls . . . Have you got all that in your head?

FRIEND: Yes.

YOU: I thought so.

YOU: How do you spell "fish"?

FRIEND: F-I-S-H.

YOU: Wrong. You spell it G-H-O-T-I.

FRIEND: That's ridiculous.

YOU: No, it isn't.
Gh in enou*gh* sounds life *f*.
O in w*o*men sounds like *i*.
Ti in informa*ti*on sounds like *sh*.
So *ghoti* spells "fish."

YOU: If I have twenty-six sheep and one dies, how many are left?

FRIEND: Twenty-five.

YOU: Wrong. Nineteen. I asked, "If I had twenty sick sheep . . ."

YOU: Can you stand on one hand and hold your tongue
with the other at the same time?

FRIEND: No.

YOU: Well, I can.

*(Here's how: Put one hand under your foot [that's standing on one
hand], then hold your tongue with the other.)*

YOU: Can you stick out your tongue and touch your
nose?

FRIEND: Nope.

YOU: I can. It's easy.

*(Here's how: Stick out your tongue while touching your nose with
your finger.)*

Ask a friend to write something on paper. Then say,
"Put it on the floor and stand on it so I can't see it." Then
say, "I bet I can tell you what's on it." Your friend says,
"No, you can't." You say, "Yes, I can. Your foot is on it."

You will need a helper for this trick. Instruct the people in the room to think of some object in the room and whisper it to your helper after you leave the room. When you return, your helper goes around the room touching things and asking, "Is it this?" You say no to everything, until he touches the right object. Then you say, "I can read your mind. This is the correct object."

How did you know? You have instructed your helper to touch every wrong object lightly and remove his hand at once. But when he touches the right object, he leaves his hand on it for a while. You notice it, but no one else will.

# Missing Finger Trick

Fold your hands, making sure your left index finger is on top. Then put your right ring finger against your left palm, like this:

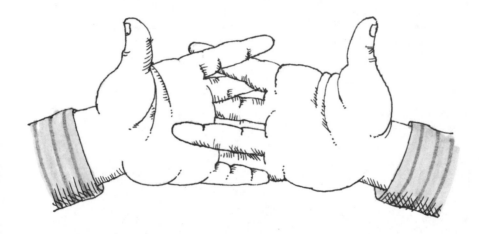

Move your right pinky between your left ring finger and left pinky, so your hands look like this:

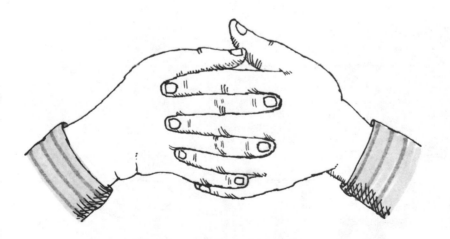

YOU: How many fingers do I have?
FRIEND: Ten.
YOU: No, I have nine. Count them if you don't believe me.

### Hink-Pinks

You think of two rhyming words, such as "ape cape." Tell your friend a definition of the words, such as "gorilla's cloak." Your friend has to guess your hink-pink. If she does, it's her turn to ask you one. Some more hink-pinks:

library corner: book nook
rodent's dwelling: mouse house
two grizzlies: bear pair

### Hinky-pinkies *(These have two syllables.)*

thin, small horse: bony pony
talking parrot: wordy birdy
different parent: other mother

## Squiggles

A drawing game for two or more people. One person draws a line or squiggle on paper. Someone else must make the mark into a picture.

## Get-to-the-Top *(A pencil-and-paper game for two people.)*

Draw any number of steps and write "TOP." One player takes $x$'s and the other takes $o$'s. Start at the bottom.

On each turn, each player must make three marks altogether. You may put three marks in one step. Or two marks in one step and one mark in another step. Or one mark in each of three steps *(see picture)*.

The first player to make a mark in the "TOP" space is the winner.

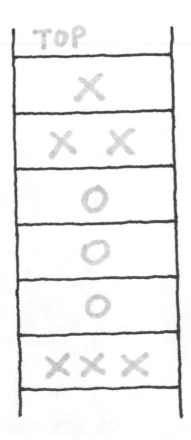

## Fill-in Stories

Don't read the story first. Instead, read the word list slowly to one or more friends. As you read, each player must write on a piece of paper the kind of word you ask for. For instance, if you say "plural noun," one player might write "apples" and another might write "feet."

You then read the story aloud. The first time you read it, the first player supplies the missing words from his list. For instance, you read, "Joe and Mary met under a _____," and your friend chimes in with the first word on his list, say "tree," or maybe "bathtub."

Each reading of the story will be funny in a different way.

### School Daze

Bill's teacher, Miss \_\_1\_\_, was very strict. One day she asked Bill, "Who is the President's wife?" Bill said, "\_\_2\_\_."

"I will flunk you," said the teacher. "You are the worst \_\_3\_\_ in the class."

Luckily Bill was able to make up for his mistake by writing an extra report on \_\_4\_\_.

Word list

1. a food _____
2. a person _____
3. singular noun _____
4. plural noun _____

## Love Story

Joe and Mary first met under a ___1___, where they had stopped to eat ___2___. When Joe saw how ___3___ Mary was, he fell head over ___4___ in love with her. "Will you marry me?" he asked, his heart full of ___5___. "Yes," said Mary, "if you promise never to ___6___ at the breakfast table." So they were wed, and had six children, all of them ___7___.

Word list

1. singular noun _____
2. plural noun _____
3. adjective _____
4. plural noun _____
5. plural noun _____
6. verb, present tense _____
7. adjective _____

## Fossil Fable

Dinosaurs lived in prehistoric times, about ___1___ years ago. Some dinosaurs looked like ___2___ and ate nothing but ___3___. But others spent their days ___4___ on ___5___. Because of this, all dinosaurs died out, and were eventually replaced by ___6___.

Word List

1. a number _____
2. plural noun _____
3. plural noun _____
4. -ing word _____
5. plural noun _____
6. plural noun _____

Make a paper Fortune Teller and tell your friends what's in store for them.

*To Make the Fortune Teller:*

1. You will need a plain square of paper. To make a square from an 8½" × 11" piece of paper, take the top right corner and pull it over to the left until the top edge of the paper is even with the left edge. Fold as shown.

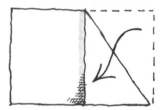

2. Cut off the paper that remains outside the folded triangle.

3. Open the triangle. Now you have a square.
4. Fold each corner of the square to the center point of your paper.

5. Turn the new square over and repeat step 4.
6. Fold this square in half.

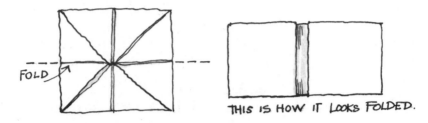

FOLD

THIS IS HOW IT LOOKS FOLDED.

7. Slip the thumb and index finger of each hand under the flaps. Press hands together, as shown.

The four sections of the Fortune Teller will close and there will be a point in the middle, like this:

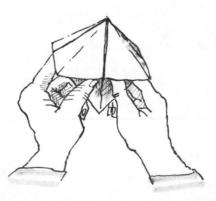

Turn the page.

*To Finish the Fortune Teller:*

8. With the Fortune Teller opened flat again, color each of the four squares a different color, or write the name of a color on each square, as shown.

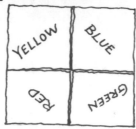

9. Now turn the Fortune Teller over. Write a number on each of the eight triangles.

10. Lift the flaps. Write a fortune in each section. Here are some ideas for fortunes:

    You are cute.
    Somebody likes you.
    You will get hard homework today.
    You are smart.
    Bad luck tomorrow.

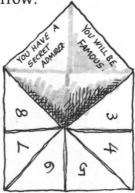

11. Now fold the Fortune Teller up again and insert thumbs and fingers as before.

*To use the Fortune Teller:*

12. Ask a friend to pick a color.

13. Spell the color, opening and closing the Fortune Teller as you spell. For instance, if your friend picks "blue," you say "B" and open the Fortune Teller to the sides. Then you close it and say "L," opening the Fortune Teller to the front and back. And so on, as shown.

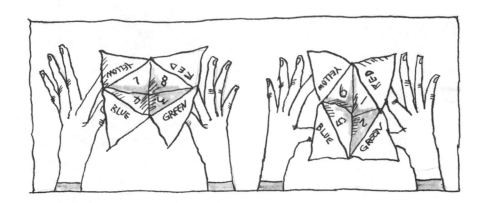

14. On the last letter, hold the Fortune Teller open and ask your friend to pick a number. Then count up to that number, opening and closing the Fortune Teller as above.

15. On the last number, hold the Fortune Teller open and ask your friend to pick another number.

16. Lift the flap of that number and read your friend's fortune.

## Palindromes

A palindrome is a word, phrase, or sentence that spells the same thing backward or forward. For example, the words "Mom" and "Pop" are both palindromes. So are all the phrases below. Check them out and make sure. (The letters stay the same, but the spacing and punctuation may change.)

'Tis Ivan on a visit.

Madam, I'm Adam.

A man, a plan, a canal, Panama!

Live not on evil.

Repaid diaper.

Lepers repel.

Was it a rat I saw.

No lemon, no melon.

Dennis sinned.

Put it up.

Enid and Nadine.

We sew.

Too hot to hoot.

Snip pins.

## Anagrams

An anagram is a word or phrase that is made up of the letters of another word or phrase. For instance, "pots" is an anagram of "spot"—both words are made of the letters *o, t, s,* and *p.* Here are some other anagram pairs.

Enraged.
Angered.

The countryside.
No city dust here.

The eyes.
They see.

Slot machines.
Cash lost in 'em.

One hug.
Enough?

A trip around the world.
Hard to plan wider tour.

Can You Make some PALINDROMES and ANAGRAMS of Your Own?

## Hand Shadows

All you need is a light and a wall to make these shady animals.

BULLS HEAD.

A BLACK SWAN.

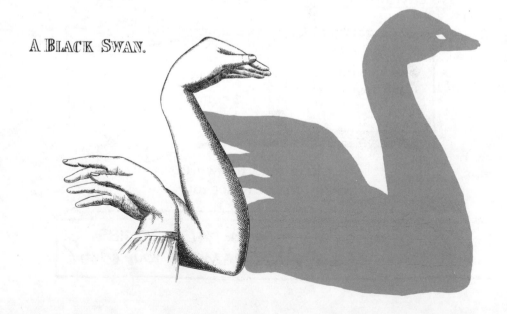

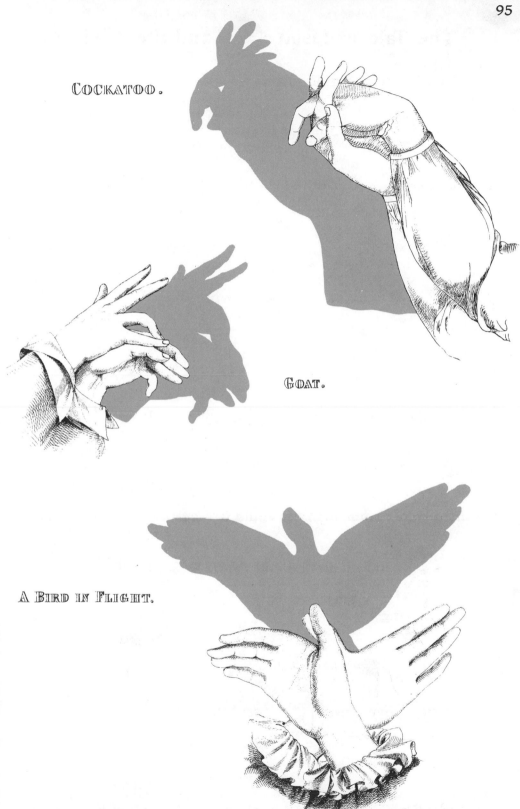

COCKATOO.

GOAT.

A BIRD IN FLIGHT.

# The Tale of Jason  and the 3 Wishes

**A Rebus**
**by Madeleine Edmondson**

Once  's mother and father  their  to

visit his  . But the very first  , he began to look

 . His voice was   . He sneezed, "A- ."

 called the doctor, who said, "Put him 2 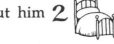 .

Give him this  .  soon be  ."

Lying in  was  fun.  was

 . Suddenly he heard a noise. The  was a-  .

Someone had come in. Who could it  ?

 looked around and  a tiny  . The

was dr-  -ing  's  .

" 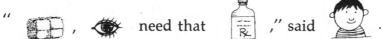 , need that  ," said  .

" love pink  ," said the  .

"Give it 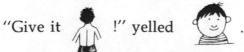 !" yelled .

"It's gone," said the  , "but I'll give

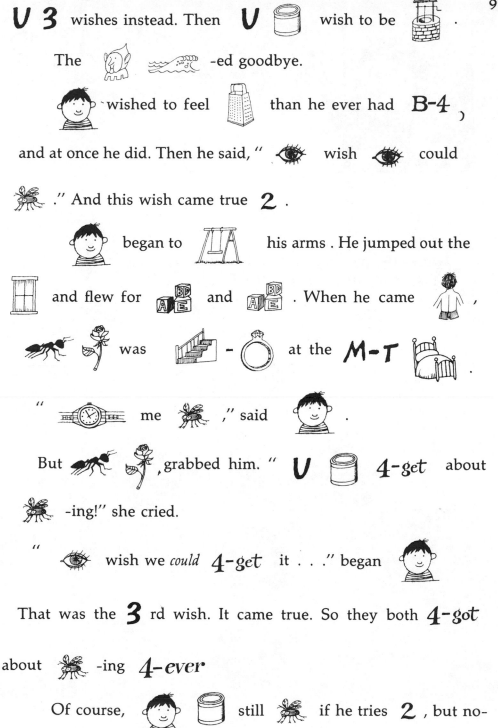

U 3 wishes instead. Then U 🥫 wish to be 🏚 .

The 🧝 🌊 -ed goodbye.

👦 wished to feel 🧀 than he ever had B-4 ,

and at once he did. Then he said, " 👁 wish 👁 could

🦟 ." And this wish came true 2 .

👦 began to 🛝 his arms . He jumped out the

🪟 and flew for 🧱 and 🧱 . When he came 🧒 ,

🐜 🌹 was 🪜 - 💍 at the M-T 🛏 .

" ⌚ me 🦟 ," said 👦 .

But 🐜 🌹 ,grabbed him. " U 🥫 4-get about

🦟 -ing!" she cried.

" 👁 wish we *could* 4-get it . . ." began 👦

That was the 3 rd wish. It came true. So they both 4-got

about 🦟 -ing 4-ever

Of course, 👦 🥫 still 🦟 if he tries 2 , but no-

body 👃 that—except the 🧝

(Solution to Rebus on page 291.)

## Penny Puzzles

1. Place six pennies the way they are shown in the picture. By moving only one penny, can you make two rows that are three pennies long?

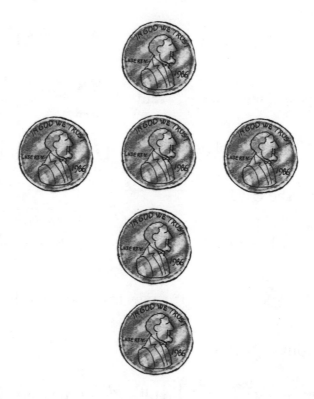

2. Put ten pennies as shown. By moving only three pennies, can you make the triangle turn upside down?

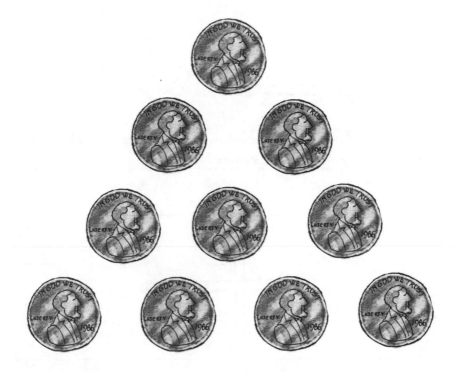

(Solutions to Penny Puzzles on page 292.)

### Matchstick Puzzles

1. Place twelve matches the way they are shown in the picture. By moving only two matches, can you spell the word "love"?

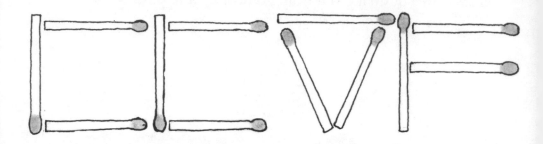

2. Place four matches as shown. By moving only one match can you make a square?

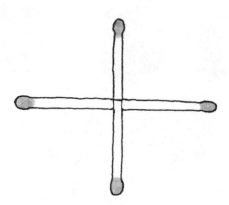

3. Place six matches as shown. Can you make nine by adding five matches?

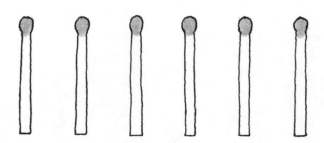

(Solutions to Matchstick Puzzles on page 293.)

## No Exit

A girl was in a room with no exit. All she had was a mirror and a table. How could she escape?

Solution:

She looked in the mirror and she saw what she saw. She took the saw and sawed the table in half. Two halves make a (w)hole, and she crawled out through it.

## Fathers and Sons

Two fathers and two sons divided three oranges among themselves. Each got exactly one orange. How is this possible?

Solution:

The two fathers and two sons were a man, his son, and his grandson.
There were only three people.

To read the solutions, hold this page up to a mirror.

### Grunchies

Here are some Grunchies. They are weird, but they all have something in common.

These things are weird too. But not one of them is a Grunchie.

Can you figure out which of these are Grunchies?

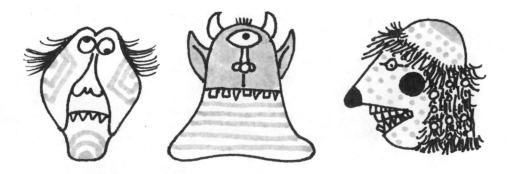

(Solution to Grunchies on page 293.)

## Write 100

Can you write "100" just as you see it here, with no numbers touching, but without lifting your pencil?

(Solution to Write 100 on page 294.)

These three codes are easy for you and your friends to learn, but hard for others to read.

NUMBER CODE: Every letter of the alphabet has a number. A is 1, B is 2, C is 3, and so on. You write in numbers, instead of letters. 2-1-4 spells "bad." What does 7-15-15-4 spell? (If you get the answer, you're pretty good.)

BACKWARD CODE: Just spell every word backward. *Terces edoc* is *secret code.* What does this message say?

Siht si delleps drawkcab.

ADD-THREE CODE: The code for each letter is three letters forward in the alphabet: A is D, B is E, C is F and so on. When you get to the end of the alphabet, start at the beginning again: X is A, Y is B, and Z is C. *Fdw* spells "cat." *Crr* spells "zoo." What does this spell?

Brx duh suhwwb vpduw!

(Solution to Secret Codes on page 294.)

LAUGHING GAS

4

Funny Stories

# The First Worm
## by Thomas Rockwell

*Would you eat fifteen worms to win a fifty-dollar bet? Billy wants to buy a minibike so badly, he's going to try. With his pal, Tom, as his coach, Billy tackles the first worm served by opponents Alan and Joe.*

The huge night crawler sprawled limply in the center of the platter, brown and steaming.

"Boiled," said Tom. "We boiled it."

Billy stormed about the barn, kicking barrels and posts, arguing. "A night crawler isn't a *worm!* If it was a worm, it'd be called a worm. A night crawler's a night crawler."

Finally Joe ran off to get his father's dictionary:

**night crawler** *n:* EARTHWORM; *esp:* a large earthworm found on the soil surface at night

Billy kicked a barrel. It still wasn't fair; he didn't care what any dictionary said; everybody knew the difference between a night crawler and a worm—look at the thing. Yergh! It was as big as a souvenir pencil from the Empire State Building! Yugh! He poked it with his finger.

"You can't quit now," said Tom. "Look at them." He nodded at Alan and Joe, waiting beside the orange crates. "They'll tell everybody you were chicken. It'll be all over school. Come on."

He led Billy back to the orange crates, sat him down, tied the napkin around his neck.

Alan flourished the knife and fork.

"Would monshure like eet carved lingthvise or crussvise?"

"Kitchip?" asked Joe, showing his teeth.

"Cut it out," said Tom. "Here." He glopped ketchup and mustard and horseradish on the night crawler, squeezed on a few drops of lemon juice, and salted and peppered it.

Billy closed his eyes and opened his mouth. "Ou woot in."

Tom sliced off the end of the night crawler and forked it up. But just as he was about to poke it into Billy's open mouth, Billy closed his mouth and opened his eyes.

"No, let me do it."

Tom handed him the fork. Billy gazed at the dripping ketchup and mustard, thinking, Awrgh! It's all right talking about eating worms, but *doing* it!?!

Tom whispered in his ear. "Minibike."

"Glug." Billy poked the fork into his mouth, chewed furiously, *gulped!* . . . *gulped!* . . . His eyes crossed, swam, squinched shut. He flapped his arms wildly. And then, opening his eyes, he grinned beatifically up at Tom.

"Superb, Gaston."

Tom cut another piece, ketchuped, mustarded, salted, peppered, horseradished, and lemoned it, and handed the fork to Billy. Billy slugged it down, smacking his lips. And so they proceeded, now sprinkling on cinnamon and sugar or a bit of cheese, some cracker crumbs or Worcestershire sauce, until there was nothing on the plate but a few stray dabs of ketchup and mustard.

"Vell," said Billy, standing up and wiping his mouth with his napkin. "So. Ve are done mit de first curse. Naw seconds?"

"Lemme look in your mouth," said Alan.

"Yeah," said Joe. "See if he swallowed it all."

"Soitinly, soitinly," said Billy. "Luke as long as you vant."

Alan and Joe scrutinized the inside of his mouth.

"Okay, okay," said Tom. "Leave him alone now. Come on. One down, fourteen to go."

"How'd it taste?" asked Alan.

"Gute, gute," said Billy. "Ver'fine, ver'fine. Hoo hoo." He flapped his arms like a big bird and began to hop around the barn, crying, "Gute, gute. Ver'fine, ver'fine. Gute, gute."

Alan and Joe and Tom looked worried.

"Uh, yeah—gute, gute. How you feeling, Billy?" Tom asked.

"Yeah, stop flapping around and come tell us how you're feeling," said Joe.

They huddled together by the orange crates as Billy hopped around and around them, flapping his arms.

"Gute, gute. Ver'fine, ver'fine. Hoo hoo."

Alan whispered, "He's crackers."

Joe edged toward the door. "Don't let him see we're afraid. Crazy people are like dogs. If they see you're afraid, they'll attack."

"It couldn't *be*," whispered Tom, standing his ground. "One worm?"

"Gute, gute," screeched Billy, hopping higher and higher and drooling from the mouth.

"Come *on*," whispered Joe to Tom.

"Hey, *Billy!*" burst out Tom suddenly in a hearty, quavering voice. "Cut it out, will you? I want to ask you something."

Billy's arms flapped slower. He tiptoed menacingly around Tom, his head cocked on one side, his cheeks puffed out. Tom hugged himself, chuckling nervously.

"Heh, heh. Cut it out, will you, Billy? Heh, heh."

Billy pounced. Joe and Alan fled, the barn door banging behind them. Billy rolled on the floor, helpless with laughter.

Tom clambered up, brushing himself off.

"Did you see their *faces?*" Billy said, laughing. "Climbing over each other out the door? Oh! Geez! Joe was pale as an onion."

"Yeah," said Tom. "Ha, ha. You fooled them."

"Ho! Geez!" Billy sat up. Then he crawled over to the door and peered out through a knothole. "Look at them, peeking up over the stone wall. Watch this."

The door swung slowly open.

Screeching, Billy hopped onto the doorsill!—into the yard!—up onto a stump!—splash into a puddle!—flapping his arms, rolling his head.

Alan and Joe galloped up the hill through the high grass, yelling, "Here he comes! Get out of the way!"

And then Billy stopped hopping, and climbing up on the stump, called in a shrill, girlish voice, "Oh, boy-oys, where are you go-ing? Id somefing tare you, iddle boys?"

Alan and Joe stopped and looked back.

"Id oo doughing home, iddle boys?" yelled Billy. "Id oo tared?"

"Who's scared, you lunk?" called Alan.

"Yeah," yelled Joe. "I guess I can go home without being called scared, if I want to."

"But ain't oo in a dawful hur-ry?" shouted Billy.

"I just remembered I was supposed to help my mother wash windows this afternoon," said Alan. "That's all." He turned and started up through the meadow, his hands in his pockets.

"Yeah," said Joe. "Me, too." He trudged after Alan.

# It's So Nice to Have a Wolf Around the House

by Harry Allard
Illustrated by James Marshall

Once upon a time there was an old man who lived alone with his three old pets. There was his dog Peppy, who was very old. There was his cat Ginger, who was very, very old. And there was Lightning, his tropical fish, who was so old that she could barely swim and preferred to float.

One day the Old Man called his three pets together and said to them, "The trouble, my friends, is that we are all so very old." Peppy wagged his tail in agreement, but just barely; Ginger twitched her ears in agreement, but just barely; and Lightning waved her fin but fell over backward because of the effort involved.

"What we need," the Old Man continued, "is a charming companion—someone to take care of us and pep us up." Lightning and Ginger and Peppy thought the Old Man was right. But this time they were too tired to wag, twitch, or wave in agreement.

That very day the Old Man put an ad in the newspaper: *Wanted: A charming companion.* [Signed] *The Old Man.*

Early the next morning a furry stranger knocked on the Old Man's door. He had long white teeth and long black nails. Handing the old man an engraved visiting card, he introduced himself. "Cuthbert Q. Devine, at your service," he said, tipping his hat. "Did you advertise for a charming companion, Old Man?"

"Yes I did," the Old Man said.

"Look no further! I am the very one you have been searching for." Cuthbert smiled from ear to ear. "Many people think that I am a wolf. That, of course, is nonsense, utter nonsense. As a matter of fact, I happen to be a dog—a German shepherd to be exact." And Cuthbert laughed in a deep, wolfish voice.

The Old Man was completely dazzled by Cuthbert Q. Devine's charming personality. He particularly liked his big bright smile. And because the Old Man's eyesight was not what it used to be, he did not see Cuthbert for what he really was—a wolf!

"You're hired," the Old Man said. And Cuthbert Q. Devine moved in, bag and baggage.

Cuthbert had not been on the job twenty-four hours before the Old Man and his three pets wondered how they had ever managed without him. First up and last to bed, Cuthbert cleaned and cooked and paid the bills. He took Peppy for long walks. He groomed Ginger and introduced her to the use of catnip. He fixed up Lightning's aquarium. He was a whiz at making fancy desserts. He massaged the Old Man's toes. He played the viola. And every Saturday night he organized a fancy costume party.

If the Old Man had ever had any doubts about Cuthbert, they were all gone now. Cuthbert had a heart of gold. All he wanted to do was to make the Old Man and his three pets happy.

But it was all too good to last.

Late one afternoon, after Cuthbert had tucked him into his easy chair and handed him his paper, the Old Man read a terrible thing right on page one: *Wanted for Bank Robbery,* the headline said. There was a picture of a wolf in a prison uniform. It was Cuthbert! The Old Man could not believe his eyes.

"To think I hired him as a charming companion, and he was a wolf the whole time!" The Old Man could not get over it. He was hurt . . . and frightened, too.

Pale and shaking, the Old Man confronted Cuthbert in the kitchen. He waved the newspaper in Cuthbert's face. "And you told me you were a German shepherd," he said.

Cuthbert's spoon clattered to the kitchen floor.

"I'm no good," he sobbed. "No good at all. But I can't help it—I've never had a chance. I always wanted to be good, but everyone expected me to be bad because I'm a wolf."

And before the Old Man could say another word, Cuthbert fainted dead away.

Somehow Ginger and Peppy and the Old Man managed to drag Cuthbert to his bed. When the doctor arrived, he said that Cuthbert had had a bad attack of nerves and would have to stay in bed for months if he were ever to get well again. "You've got a very sick wolf on your hands," the doctor told the Old Man as he left.

Now it was the Old Man who got up early to clean and cook and pay the bills. But he did not mind at all— in fact he felt years younger. Peppy helped, and so did Ginger.

With so much to do for Cuthbert, Peppy forgot his aches and pains; and everyone said that Ginger was as frisky as a kitten again. Lightning did her share, too: She spent her days blowing beautiful bubbles to amuse Cuthbert—it seemed to soothe his frayed nerves.

Cuthbert had to stay in bed for a long time, but at last he was well enough to get up. One day he told the Old Man how ashamed he was of robbing all those banks. He asked the Old Man what he should do.

On the Old Man's advice, Cuthbert turned himself in to the police. When his case came to court, Cuthbert promised the judge that he would never rob a bank again. The judge believed him and said, "I will let you go this time because you have done so much for the Old Man and his pets."

The Old Man was very happy. So was Cuthbert, and his paws shook from relief.

Cuthbert finally got completely well and lived with the Old Man and his three pets for the rest of their lives. As a matter of fact, all five of them are still living in Arizona to this day. The Old Man moved there with Lightning and Ginger and Peppy because the desert climate was better for Cuthbert's health.

*Mrs. Pepperpot is an old woman who shrinks to a tiny size at the oddest moments. Usually she keeps her shrinking a secret, but this is hard to do in the middle of an exciting ski race.*

Mr. Pepperpot had decided to go in for the annual local ski race. He had been a pretty good skier when he was young, so he said to Mrs. Pepperpot:

"I don't see why I shouldn't have a go this year; I feel more fit than I have for many years."

"That's right, husband, you do that," said Mrs. Pepperpot, "and if you win the cup you'll get your favorite ginger cake when you come home."

So Mr. Pepperpot put his name down, and when the day came he put on his white parka and blue cap with a pompon on the top and strings under his chin. He slung his skis over his shoulders and said he would wax them when he got to the starting point.

"Best of luck!" said Mrs. Pepperpot. She was already greasing the cake pan and stoking the stove for her baking.

"Thanks, wife," said Mr. Pepperpot and went off. It was not before he had turned the corner by the main road that Mrs. Pepperpot caught sight of his can of wax, which he had left on the sideboard.

"What a dunderhead that man is!" exclaimed Mrs. Pepperpot. "Now I shall have to go after him, I suppose; otherwise his precious skis are more likely to go backward than forward and there'll be no cup in this house today."

So Mrs. Pepperpot flung her shawl around her shoulders and trotted up the road as fast as she could with the can of wax. When she got near the starting point there was a great crowd gathered. She dodged in and out to try and find her husband, but everyone seemed to be wearing white parkas and blue caps. At last she saw a pair of sticks stuck in the snow with a blue cap hanging from the top. She could see the initials "P.P." sewn in red thread inside.

"That must be his cap," thought Mrs. Pepperpot. "Those are his initials—Peter Pepperpot. I sewed them on myself in red thread like that. I'll just drop the wax in the cap; then he'll find it when he comes to pick up his sticks."

As she bent forward to put the wax in the cap, she accidentally knocked it off the stick and at that moment she shrank so quickly that it was she who fell into the cap, while the can of wax rolled out into the snow!

"No harm done," thought Mrs. Pepperpot. "When he comes along he'll see me in his cap. Then he can put me down somewhere out of the way of the race. And as soon as I grow large again, I can go home."

But a moment later a big hand reached down, snatched up the cap, and crammed it over a mop of thick hair. The strings were firmly tied and Mrs. Pepperpot was trapped!

"Oh well!" she thought. "I'd better not say anything before the race starts." For she knew Mr. Pepperpot hated to think anybody might get to know about her shrinking.

"Number Forty-six!" she heard the starter shout. "On your mark, get set, go!" And Number Forty-six, with Mrs. Pepperpot in his cap, glided off to a smooth start.

"Somebody must have lent him some wax," she thought; "there's nothing wrong with his skis, anyway." Then from under the cap she shouted, "Don't overdo it, now, or you'll have no breath left for the spurt at the end!"

She could feel the skier slow up a little. "I suppose you know who's under your cap?" she added. "You had forgotten the wax, so I brought it along. Only I fell into your cap instead of the wax."

Mrs. Pepperpot now felt the skier's head turn around to see if anyone was talking to him from behind.

"It's me, you fool!" said Mrs. Pepperpot. "I've shrunk again. You'll have to put me off by the lane to our house —you pass right by, remember?"

But the skier had stopped completely now.

"Come on, man, get a move on!" shouted Mrs. Pepperpot. "They'll all be passing you!"

"Is it . . . is it true that you're the little old woman who shrinks to the size of a pepperpot?"

"Of course—you know that!" laughed Mrs. Pepperpot.

"Am *I* married to *you?* Is it *my* wife who shrinks?"

"Yes, yes, but hurry now!"

"No," said the skier, "if that's how it is, I'm not going on with the race at all."

"Rubbish!" shouted Mrs. Pepperpot. "You *must* go on! I put a cake in the oven before I went out and if it's scorched it'll be all your fault!"

But the skier didn't budge.

"Maybe you'd like me to pop out of your cap and show myself to everybody? Any minute now I might go back to my full size and then the cap will burst and the whole crowd will see who is married to the shrinking woman. Come on, now! With any luck you may just do it, but there's no time to lose. Hurry!"

This worked; the skier shot off at full speed, helping himself to huge strides with his sticks. "Track!" he shouted as he sped past the other skiers. But when they came to the refreshment stand Mrs. Pepperpot could smell the lovely hot soup, and she thought her husband deserved a break. "We're way ahead now," she called. "You could take a rest."

The skier slowed down to a stop and Mrs. Pepperpot could hear there were many people standing around him. "Well done!" they said. "You're very well placed. But what are you looking so worried about? Surely you're not frightened of the last lap, are you?"

"No, no, nothing like that!" said the skier. "It's this cap of mine—I'm dead scared of my cap!"

But the people patted him on the back and told him not to worry, he had a good chance of winning.

Under the cap Mrs. Pepperpot was getting restless again. "That's enough of that!" she called. "We'll have to go on now!"

The people who stood nearest heard the voice and wondered who spoke. The woman who ladled out the soup said, "Probably some loudspeaker."

And Mrs. Pepperpot couldn't help laughing. "Nearer the truth than you think!" she thought. Then she called out again, "Come on, husband, put that spurt on, and let's see if we can make it!"

And the skis shot away again, leaping many yards each time the sticks struck into the snow. Very soon Mrs. Pepperpot could hear the sound of clapping and cheering.

"What do we do now?" whispered the skier in a miserable voice. "Can you last another minute? Then I can throw the cap off under the fir trees just before we reach the finishing line."

"Yes, that will be all right," said Mrs. Pepperpot. And, as the skis sped down the last slope, the strings were untied and the cap flew through the air, landing safely under the fir trees.

When Mrs. Pepperpot had rolled over and over many times she found herself growing big once more. So she got up, shook the snow off her skirt, and walked quietly home to her house. From the cheering in the distance she was sure her husband had won the cup.

The cake was only a little bit burnt on the top when she took it out of the oven, so she cut off the black part and gave it to the cat. Then she whipped some cream to put on top and made a steaming pot of coffee to have ready for her champion husband.

Sure enough, Mr. Pepperpot soon came home—*without* the cup. "I forgot to take the wax," he said, "so I didn't think it was worth going in for the race. But I watched it, and you should have seen Paul Petersen today; I've never seen him run like that in all my born days. All the same, he looked very queer, as if he'd seen a ghost or something. When it was over he kept talking about his wife and his cap, and he wasn't satisfied till he'd telephoned his house and made sure his wife had been there all the time, watching the race on television."

Then Mrs. Pepperpot began to laugh. And ever since, when she's feeling sad or things are not going just right, all she has to do is to remember the day she went ski-racing in the wrong cap, and then she laughs and laughs and laughs.

# The Twits

## by Roald Dahl

*How would you like to finish your milk one day and find a glass eye staring up at you? Or maybe you'd prefer a Giant Skillywiggler in your bed or a juicy surprise in your spaghetti. Those are just a few of the wicked tricks the world's most horrible couple have played on each other. Here is one more you won't forget.*

## The Funny Walking Stick

To pay Mrs. Twit back for the worms in his spaghetti, Mr. Twit thought up a really clever nasty trick.

One night, when the old woman was asleep, he crept out of bed and took her walking stick downstairs to his workshed. There he stuck a tiny round piece of wood (no thicker than a penny) onto the bottom of the stick.

This made the stick longer, but the difference was so small, the next morning Mrs. Twit didn't notice it.

The following night, Mr. Twit stuck on another tiny bit of wood. Every night, he crept downstairs and added an extra tiny thickness of wood to the end of the walking stick. He did it very neatly so that the extra bits looked like a part of the old stick.

Gradually, but oh so gradually, Mrs. Twit's walking stick was getting longer and longer.

Now, when something is growing very very slowly, it is almost impossible to notice it happening. You yourself, for example, are actually growing taller every day that goes by, but you wouldn't think it, would you? It's happening so slowly you can't even notice it from one week to the next.

It was the same with Mrs. Twit's walking stick. It was all so slow and gradual that she didn't notice how long it was getting even when it was halfway up to her shoulder.

"That stick's too long for you," Mr. Twit said to her one day.

"Why so it is!" Mrs. Twit said, looking at the stick. "I've had a feeling there was something wrong, but I couldn't for the life of me think what it was."

"There's something wrong all right," Mr. Twit said, beginning to enjoy himself.

"What *can* have happened?" Mrs. Twit said, staring at her old walking stick. "It must suddenly have grown longer."

"Don't be a fool!" Mr. Twit said. "How can a walking stick possibly grow longer? It's made of dead wood, isn't it? Dead wood can't grow."

"Then what on earth has happened?" cried Mrs. Twit.

"It's not the stick, it's *you!*" said Mr. Twit, grinning horribly. "It's *you* that's getting *shorter!* I've been noticing it for some time now."

"That's not true!" cried Mrs. Twit.

"You're shrinking, woman!" said Mr. Twit.

"It's not possible!"

"Oh yes it jolly well is," said Mr. Twit. "You're shrinking fast! You're shrinking *dangerously* fast! Why, you must have shrunk at least a foot in the last few days!"

"Never!" she cried.

"Of course you have! Take a look at your stick, you old goat, and see how much you've shrunk in comparison! You've got the *shrinks,* that's what you've got! You've got the dreaded *shrinks!*"

Mrs. Twit began to feel so trembly she had to sit down.

As soon as Mrs. Twit sat down, Mr. Twit pointed at her and shouted, "There you are! You're sitting in your old chair and you've shrunk so much your feet aren't even touching the ground!"

Mrs. Twit looked down at her feet and by golly the man was right. Her feet were not touching the ground.

Mr. Twit, you see, had been just as clever with the chair as he'd been with the walking stick. Every night when he had gone downstairs and stuck a little bit extra onto the stick, he had done the same to the four legs of Mrs. Twit's chair.

"Just look at you sitting there in your same old chair," he cried, "and you've shrunk so much your feet are dangling in the air!"

Mrs. Twit went white with fear.

"You've got the *shrinks!*" cried Mr. Twit, pointing his finger at her like a pistol. "You've got them badly! You've got the most terrible case of shrinks I've ever seen!"

Mrs. Twit became so frightened she began to dribble. But Mr. Twit, still remembering the worms in his spaghetti, didn't feel sorry for her at all. "I suppose you know what *happens* to you when you get the shrinks?" he said.

"What?" gasped Mrs. Twit. "What happens?"

"Your head SHRINKS into your neck . . .

"And your neck SHRINKS into your body . . .

"And your body SHRINKS into your legs . . .

"And your legs SHRINK into your feet. And in the end there's nothing left except a pair of shoes and a bundle of old clothes."

"I can't bear it!" cried Mrs. Twit.

"It's a terrible disease," said Mr. Twit. "The worst in the world."

"How long have I got?" cried Mrs. Twit. "How long before I finish up as a bundle of old clothes and a pair of shoes?"

Mr. Twit put on a very solemn face. "At the rate you're going," he said, shaking his head sadly, "I'd say not more than ten or eleven days."

"But isn't there *anything* we can do?" cried Mrs. Twit.

"There's only one cure for the shrinks," said Mr. Twit.

"Tell me!" she cried. "Oh, tell me quickly!"

"We'll have to hurry!" said Mr. Twit.

"I'm ready. I'll hurry! I'll do anything you say!" cried Mrs. Twit.

"You won't last long if you don't," said Mr. Twit, giving her another grizzly grin.

"What is it I must do?" cried Mrs. Twit, clutching her cheeks.

"You've got to be *stretched,*" said Mr. Twit.

Mr. Twit led Mrs. Twit outdoors, where he had everything ready for the great stretching.

He had one hundred balloons and lots of string.

He had a gas cylinder for filling the balloons.

He had fixed an iron ring into the ground.

"Stand here," he said, pointing to the iron ring. He then tied Mrs. Twit's ankles to the iron ring.

When that was done, he began filling the balloons with gas. Each balloon was on a long string and when it was filled with gas it pulled on its string, trying to go up and up. Mr. Twit tied the ends of the strings to the top half of Mrs. Twit's body. Some he tied around her neck, some under her arms, some to her wrists, and some even to her hair.

Soon there were fifty colored balloons floating in the air above Mrs. Twit's head.

"Can you feel them stretching you?" asked Mr. Twit.

"I can! I can!" cried Mrs. Twit. "They're stretching me like mad."

He put on another ten balloons. The upward pull became very strong.

Mrs. Twit was quite helpless now. With her feet tied to the ground and her arms pulled upward by the balloons, she was unable to move. She was a prisoner, and Mr. Twit had intended to go away and leave her like that for a couple of days and nights to teach her a lesson. In fact, he was just about to leave when Mrs. Twit opened her big mouth and said something silly.

"Are you sure my feet are tied properly to the ground?" she gasped. "If those strings around my ankles break, it'll be goodbye for me!"

And that's what gave Mr. Twit his second nasty idea . . .

# THE FIRST SHLEMIEL

**by Isaac Bashevis Singer**
**Illustrated by Maurice Sendak**

*What is a shlemiel? A shlemiel is a simpleton. A shlemiel is a misfit
and a nitwit. A shlemiel is lazy and clumsy too. Here is the original
shlemiel.*

There are many shlemiels in the world, but the very first
one came from the village of Chelm. He had a wife, Mrs.
Shlemiel, and a child, Little Shlemiel, but he could not
provide for them. His wife used to get up early in the
morning to sell vegetables in the marketplace. Mr.
Shlemiel stayed at home and rocked the baby to sleep.
He also took care of the rooster which lived in the room
with them, feeding it corn and water.

Mrs. Shlemiel knew that her husband was unhandy
and lazy. He also loved to sleep and had a sweet tooth. It
so happened that one night she prepared a potful of delicious jam. The next day she worried that while she was
away at the market, her husband would eat it all up. So
before she left, she said to him, "Shlemiel, I'm going to
the market and I will be back in the evening. There are
three things that I want to tell you. Each one is very
important."

"What are they?" asked Shlemiel.

"First, make sure that the baby does not fall out of his
cradle."

"Good. I will take care of the baby."

"Secondly, don't let the rooster get out of the house."

"Good. The rooster won't get out of the house."

"Thirdly, there is a potful of poison on the shelf. Be
careful not to eat it, or you will die," said Mrs. Shlemiel,
pointing to the pot of jam she had placed high up in the
cupboard.

She had decided to fool him, because she knew that
once he tasted the delicious jam, he would not stop eating until the pot was empty. It was just before Hanuk-

kah, and she needed the jam to serve with the holiday pancakes.

As soon as his wife left, Shlemiel began to rock the baby and to sing him a lullaby:

> *I am a big Shlemiel.*
> *You are a little Shlemiel.*
> *When you grow up,*
> *You will be a big Shlemiel*
> *And I will be an old Shlemiel.*
> *When you have children,*
> *You will be a papa Shlemiel*
> *And I will be a grandpa Shlemiel.*

The baby soon fell asleep and Shlemiel dozed too, still rocking the cradle with his foot.

Shlemiel dreamed that he had become the richest man in Chelm. He was so rich that he could eat pancakes with jam not only on Hanukkah but every day of the year. He spent all day with the other wealthy men of Chelm playing games with a golden dreidel. Shlemiel knew a trick, and whenever it was his turn to spin the dreidel, it fell on the winning "G." He grew so famous that nobles from distant countries came to him and said, "Shlemiel, we want you to be our king."

Shlemiel told them he did not want to be a king. But the nobles fell on their knees before him and insisted until he had to agree. They placed a crown on his head and led him to a golden throne. Mrs. Shlemiel, now a queen, no longer needed to sell vegetables in the market. She sat next to him, and between them they shared a huge pancake spread with jam. He ate from one side and she from the other until their mouths met.

As Shlemiel sat and dreamed his sweet dream the rooster suddenly started crowing. It had a very strong voice. When it came out with a cock-a-doodle-doo, it rang like a bell. Now when a bell rang in Chelm, it usually meant there was a fire. Shlemiel awakened from his dream and jumped up in fright, overturning the cradle. The baby fell out and hurt his head. In his confusion Shlemiel ran to the window and opened it to see where the fire was. The moment he opened the window, the excited rooster flew out and hopped away.

Shlemiel called after it, "Rooster, you come back. If Mrs. Shlemiel finds you gone, she will rave and rant and I will never hear the end of it."

But the rooster paid no attention to Shlemiel. It didn't even look back, and soon it had disappeared from sight.

When Shlemiel realized that there was no fire, he closed the window and went back to the crying baby, who by this time had a big bump on his forehead from the fall. With great effort Shlemiel comforted the baby, righted the cradle, and put him back into it.

Again he began to rock the cradle and sing a song:

> In my dream I was a rich Shlemiel
> But awake I am a poor Shlemiel.
> In my dream I ate pancakes with jam;
> Awake I chew bread and onion.
> In my dream I was Shlemiel the King
> But awake I'm just Shlemiel.

Having finally sung the baby to sleep, Shlemiel began to worry about his troubles. He knew that when his wife returned and found the rooster gone and the baby with a bump on his head, she would be beside herself with anger. Mrs. Shlemiel had a very loud voice, and when she scolded and screamed, poor Shlemiel trembled with fear. Shlemiel could foresee that tonight, when she got home, his wife would be angrier than ever before and would berate him and call him names.

Suddenly Shlemiel said to himself, "What is the sense

of such a life? I'd rather be dead." And he decided to end his life. But how to do it? He then remembered what his wife had told him in the morning about the pot of poison that stood on the shelf. "That's what I will do. I will poison myself. When I'm dead she can revile me as much as she likes. A dead Shlemiel does not hear when he is screamed at."

Shlemiel was a short man and he could not reach the shelf. He got a stool, climbed up on it, took down the pot, and began to eat.

"Oh, the poison tastes sweet," he said to himself. He had heard that some poisons have a bitter taste and others are sweet. "But," he reasoned, "sweet poison is better than bitter," and proceeded to finish up the jam. It tasted so good, he licked the pot clean.

After Shlemiel had finished the pot of poison, he lay down on the bed. He was sure that the poison would soon begin to burn his insides and that he would die. But half an hour passed and then an hour, and Shlemiel lay without a single pain in his belly.

"This poison works very slowly," Shlemiel decided. He was thirsty and wanted a drink of water, but there was no water in the house. In Chelm water had to be fetched from an outside well, and Shlemiel was too lazy to go and get it.

Shlemiel remembered that his wife was saving a bottle of apple cider for the holidays. Apple cider was expensive, but when a man is about to die, what is the point of saving money? Shlemiel got out the bottle of cider and drank it down to the last drop.

Now Shlemiel began to have an ache in his stomach, and he was sure that the poison had begun to work. Convinced that he was about to die, he said to himself, "It's not really so bad to die. With such poison I wouldn't mind dying every day." And he dozed off.

He dreamed again that he was a king. He wore three crowns on his head, one on top of the other. Before him stood three golden pots: one filled with pancakes, one with jam, and one with apple cider. Whenever he soiled his beard with eating, a servant wiped it for him with a napkin.

Mrs. Shlemiel, the queen, sat next to him on her separate throne and said, "Of all the kings who ever ruled in Chelm, you are the greatest. The whole of Chelm pays homage to your wisdom. Fortunate is the queen of such a king. Happy is the prince who has you as a father."

Shlemiel was awakened by the sound of the door creaking open. The room was dark and he heard his wife's screechy voice. "Shlemiel, why didn't you light the lamp?"

"It sounds like my wife, Mrs. Shlemiel," Shlemiel said to himself. "But how is it possible that I hear her voice? I happen to be dead. Or can it be that the poison hasn't worked yet and I am still alive?" He got up, his legs shaking, and saw his wife lighting the lamp.

Suddenly she began to scream at the top of her lungs. "Just look at the baby! He has a bump on his head. Shlemiel, where is the rooster, and who drank the apple cider? Woe is me! He drank up the cider! He lost the rooster and let the baby get a bump on his head. Shlemiel, what have you done?"

"Don't scream, dear wife. I'm about to die. You will soon be a widow."

"Die? Widow? What are you talking about? You look healthy as a horse."

"I've poisoned myself," Shlemiel replied.

"Poisoned? What do you mean?" asked Mrs. Shlemiel.

"I've eaten your potful of poison."

And Shlemiel pointed to the empty pot of jam.

"Poison?" said Mrs. Shlemiel. "That's my pot of jam for Hanukkah."

"But you told me it was poison," Shlemiel insisted.

"You fool," she said. "I did that to keep you from eating it before the holiday. Now you've swallowed the whole potful." And Mrs. Shlemiel burst out crying.

Shlemiel too began to cry, but not from sorrow. He wept tears of joy that he would remain alive. The wailing of the parents woke the baby and he too began to yowl. When the neighbors heard all the crying, they came running and soon all of Chelm knew the story. The good neighbors took pity on the Shlemiels and brought them a fresh pot of jam and another bottle of apple cider. The rooster, which had gotten cold and hungry from wandering around outside, returned by itself and the Shlemiels had a happy holiday after all.

As always in Chelm when an unusual event occurred, the Elders came together to ponder over what had happened. For seven days and seven nights they sat wrinkling their foreheads and tugging at their beards, searching for the true meaning of the incident. At the end the sages all came to the same conclusion: A wife who has a child in the cradle and a rooster to take care of should never lie to her husband and tell him that a pot of jam is a pot of poison, or that a pot of poison is a pot of jam, even if he is lazy, has a sweet tooth, and is a shlemiel besides.

# Beezus and Her Little Sister, Ramona

**by Beverly Cleary**
**Illustrated by Louis Darling**

*Beezus (short for Beatrice) is a normal happy girl, but she has a problem. Her four-year-old sister, Ramona, insists that Beezus read her the same picture book about a little steam shovel named Scoopy over and over again. In self-defense, Beezus takes Ramona to the library to find another book.*

"Is this where you pay for the books?" asked Ramona.

"We don't have to pay for the books," said Beezus.

"Are you going to charge them?" Ramona asked.

Beezus pulled her library card out of her sweater pocket. "I show this card to the lady and she lets us keep the books for two weeks. A library isn't like a store, where you buy things."

Ramona looked as if she did not understand. "I want a card," she said.

"You have to be able to write your own name before you can have a library card," Beezus explained.

"I can write my name," said Ramona.

"Oh, Ramona," said Beezus, "you can't, either."

"Perhaps she really does know how to write her name," said Miss Greever, as she took a card out of her desk. Beezus watched doubtfully while Miss Greever asked Ramona her name and age. Then the librarian asked Ramona what her father's occupation was. When Ramona didn't understand, she asked, "What kind of work does your father do?"

"He mows the lawn," said Ramona promptly.

The librarian laughed. "I mean, how does he earn his living?"

Somehow Beezus did not like to have Miss Greever laugh at her little sister. After all, how could Ramona be expected to know what Father did? "He works for the Pacific Gas and Electric Company," Beezus told the librarian.

Miss Greever wrote this down on the card and shoved it across the desk to Ramona. "Write your name on this line," she directed.

Nothing daunted, Ramona grasped the pencil in her fist and began to write. She bore down so hard that the tip snapped off the lead, but she wrote on. When she laid down the pencil, Beezus picked up the card to see what she had written. The line on the card was filled with

"That's my name," said Ramona proudly.

"That's just scribbling," Beezus told her.

"It is too my name," insisted Ramona, while Miss Greever quietly dropped the card into the wastebasket. "I've watched you write and I know how."

"Here, Ramona, you can hold my card." Beezus tried to be comforting. "You can pretend it's yours."

Ramona brightened at this, and Miss Greever checked out the books on Beezus' card. As soon as they got home, Ramona demanded, "Read my new book to me."

And so Beezus began. "Big Steve was a steam shovel. He was the biggest steam shovel in the whole city . . ." When she finished the book she had to admit she liked Big Steve better than Scoopy. His only sound effects were tooting and growling. He tooted and growled in big letters on every page. Big Steve did not shed tears or want to be a pile driver. He worked hard at being a steam shovel, and by the end of the book Beezus had learned a lot about steam shovels. Unfortunately, she did not want to learn about steam shovels. Oh, well, she guessed she could stand two weeks of Big Steve.

"Read it again," said Ramona enthusiastically. "I like Big Steve. He's better than Scoopy."

"How would you like me to show you how to really write your name?" Beezus asked, hoping to divert Ramona from steam shovels.

"O.K.," agreed Ramona.

Beezus found pencil and paper and wrote *Ramona* in large, careful letters across the top of the paper.

Ramona studied it critically. "I don't like it," she said at last.

"But that's the way your name is spelled," Beezus explained.

"You didn't make dots and lines," said Ramona. Seizing the pencil, she wrote,

"But, Ramona, you don't understand." Beezus took the pencil and wrote her own name on the paper. "You've seen me write *Beatrice,* which has an *i* and a *t* in it. See, like that. You don't have an *i* or a *t* in your name, because it isn't spelled that way."

Ramona looked skeptical. She grabbed the pencil again and wrote with a flourish,

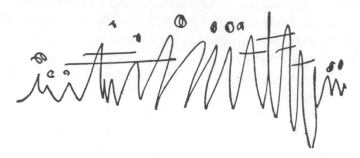

"That's my name, because I like it," she announced. "I like to make dots and lines." Lying flat on her stomach on the floor she proceeded to fill the paper with *i*'s and *t*'s.

"But, Ramona, nobody's name is spelled with just . . ." Beezus stopped. What was the use? Trying to explain spelling and writing to Ramona was too complicated. Everything became difficult when Ramona was around, even an easy thing like taking a book out of the library. Well, if Ramona was happy thinking her name was spelled with *i*'s and *t*'s, she could go ahead and think it.

The next two weeks were fairly peaceful. Mother and Father soon tired of tooting and growling and, like Beezus, they looked forward to the day *Big Steve* was due at the library. Father even tried to hide the book behind the radio, but Ramona soon found it. Beezus was happy that one part of her plan had worked—Ramona had forgotten *The Littlest Steam Shovel* now that she had a better book. On Ramona's second trip to the library, perhaps Miss Evans could find a book that would make her forget steam shovels entirely.

As for Ramona, she was perfectly happy. She had three people to read aloud a book she liked, and she spent much of her time covering sheets of paper with *i*'s and *t*'s. Sometimes she wrote in pencil, sometimes she wrote in crayon, and once she wrote in ink until her mother caught her at it.

Finally, to the relief of the rest of the family, the day came when *Big Steve* had to be returned. "Come on, Ramona," said Beezus. "It's time to go to the library for another book."

"I have a book," said Ramona, who was lying on her stomach writing her version of her name on a piece of paper with purple crayon.

"No, it belongs to the library," Beezus explained, glad that for once Ramona couldn't possibly get her own way.

"It's my book," said Ramona, crossing several *t*'s with a flourish.

"Beezus is right, dear," observed Mother. "Run along and get *Big Steve.*"

Ramona looked sulky, but she went into the bedroom. In a few minutes she appeared with *Big Steve* in her hand and a satisfied expression on her face. "It's my book," she announced. "I wrote my name in it."

Mother looked alarmed. "What do you mean, Ramona? Let me see." She took the book and opened it. Every page in the book was covered with enormous purple *i*'s and *t*'s in Ramona's very best handwriting.

"Mother!" cried Beezus. "Look what she's done! And in crayon so it won't erase."

"Ramona Quimby," said Mother. "You're a very naughty girl! Why did you do a thing like that?"

"It's my book," said Ramona stubbornly. "I like it."

"Mother, what am I going to do?" Beezus demanded. "It's checked out on my card and I'm responsible. They won't let me take any more books out of the library, and I won't have anything to read, and it will all be Ramona's fault. She's always spoiling my fun and it isn't fair!" Beezus didn't know what she would do without her library card. She couldn't get along without library books. She just couldn't, that was all.

"I do *not* spoil your fun," stormed Ramona. "You have all the fun. I can't read and it isn't fair." Ramona's words ended in a howl as she buried her face in her mother's skirt.

"I couldn't read when I was your age and I didn't have someone to read to me all the time, so it is too fair," argued Beezus. "You always get your own way, because you're the youngest."

"I do not!" shouted Ramona. "And you don't read all the time. You're mean!"

"I am *not* mean," Beezus shouted back.

"Children!" cried Mother. "Stop it, both of you! Ramona, you were a very naughty girl!" A loud sniff came from Ramona. "And, Beezus," her mother continued, "the library won't take your card away from you. If you'll get my purse I'll give you some money to pay for the damage to the book. Take Ramona along with you, explain what happened, and the librarian will tell you how much to pay."

This made Beezus feel better. Ramona sulked all the way to the library, but when they got there Beezus was pleased to see that Miss Evans, the children's librarian, was sitting behind the desk. Miss Evans was the kind of librarian who would understand about little sisters.

"Hello, Beatrice," said Miss Evans. "Is this your little sister I've heard so much about?"

Beezus wondered what Miss Evans had heard about Ramona. "Yes, this is Ramona," she said and went on hesitantly, "and, Miss Evans, she—"

"I'm a bad girl," interrupted Ramona, smiling winningly at the librarian.

"Oh, you are?" said Miss Evans. "What did you do?"

"I wrote in a book," said Ramona, not the least ashamed. "I wrote in purple crayon and it will never, never erase. Never, never, never."

Embarrassed, Beezus handed Miss Evans *Big Steve the Steam Shovel.* "Mother gave me the money to pay for the damage," she explained.

The librarian turned the pages of the book. "Well, you didn't miss a page, did you?" she finally said to Ramona.

"No," said Ramona, pleased with herself. "And it will never, never—"

"I'm awfully sorry," interrupted Beezus. "After this I'll try to keep our library books where she can't reach them."

Miss Evans consulted a file of little cards in a drawer. "Since every page in the book was damaged and the library can no longer use it, I'll have to ask you to pay for the whole book. I'm sorry, but this is the rule. It will cost two dollars and fifty cents."

Two dollars and fifty cents! What a lot of things that would have bought, Beezus reflected, as she pulled three folded dollar bills out of her pocket and handed them to the librarian. Miss Evans put the money in a drawer and gave Beezus fifty cents in change.

Then Miss Evans took a rubber stamp and stamped something inside the book. By twisting her head around, Beezus could see that the word was *Discarded.* "There!" Miss Evans said, pushing the book across the desk. "You have paid for it, so now it's yours."

Beezus stared at the librarian. "You mean . . . to keep?"

"That's right," answered Miss Evans.

Ramona grabbed the book. "It's mine. I told you it was mine!" Then she turned to Beezus and said triumphantly, "You said people didn't buy books at the library and now you just bought one!"

"Buying a book and paying for damage are not the same thing," Miss Evans pointed out to Ramona.

Beezus could see that Ramona didn't care. The book was hers, wasn't it? It was paid for and she could keep it. And that's not fair, thought Beezus. Ramona shouldn't get her own way when she had been naughty.

"But, Miss Evans," protested Beezus, "if she spoils a book she shouldn't get to keep it. Now every time she finds a book she likes she will . . ." Beezus did not go on. She knew very well what Ramona would do, but she wasn't going to say it out loud in front of her.

"I see what you mean." Miss Evans looked thoughtful. "Give me the book, Ramona," she said.

Doubtfully Ramona handed her the book.

"Ramona, do you have a library card?" Miss Evans asked.

Ramona shook her head.

"Then Beezus must have taken the book out on her card," said Miss Evans. "So the book belongs to Beezus."

Why, of course! Why hadn't she thought of that before? It was her book, not Ramona's. "Oh, thank you," said Beezus gratefully, as Miss Evans handed the book to her. She could do anything she wanted with it.

For once Ramona didn't know what to say. She scowled and looked as if she were building up to a tantrum. "You've got to read it to me," she said at last.

"Not unless I feel like it," said Beezus. "After all, it's my book," she couldn't resist adding.

"That's no fair!" Ramona looked as if she were about to howl.

"It is too fair," said Beezus calmly. "And if you have a tantrum I won't read to you at all."

Suddenly, as if she had decided Beezus meant what she said, Ramona stopped scowling. "O.K.," she said cheerfully.

Beezus watched her carefully for a minute. Yes, she really was being agreeable, thought Beezus with a great feeling of relief. And now that she did not have to read *Big Steve* unless she wanted to, Beezus felt she would not mind reading it once in a while. "Come on, Ramona," she said. "Maybe I'll have time to read to you before Father comes home."

"O.K.," said Ramona happily, as she took Beezus' hand.

Miss Evans smiled at the girls as they started to leave. "Good luck, Beatrice," she said.

# Showing Off in Sunday School
by Mark Twain

*About a hundred years ago, when Mark Twain wrote his famous book* The Adventures of Tom Sawyer, *children were expected to learn their lessons by heart and to be good all the time. Not every child was perfect, of course, but it seemed as if Tom was always in trouble. How then was it possible that this same Tom was about to win a Sunday school prize for reciting long passages from the Bible?*

The sun rose upon a tranquil world, and beamed down upon the peaceful village like a benediction. Breakfast over, Aunt Polly had family worship: it began with a prayer built from the ground up of solid courses of Scriptural quotations, welded together with a thin mortar of originality; and from the summit of this she delivered a grim chapter of the Mosaic Law, as from Sinai.

Then Tom girded up his loins, so to speak, and went to work to "get his verses." Sid had learned his lesson days before. Tom bent all his energies to the memorizing of five verses, and he chose part of the Sermon on the Mount, because he could find no verses that were shorter. At the end of half an hour Tom had a vague general idea of his lesson, but no more, for his mind was traversing the whole field of human thought, and his hands were busy with distracting recreations. His cousin Mary took his book to hear him recite, and he tried to find his way through the fog:

"Blessed are—a—a—"

"Poor—"

"Yes—poor; blessed are the poor—a—a—"

"In spirit—"

"In spirit; blessed are the poor in spirit, for they—they—"

"*Theirs*—"

"For *theirs*. Blessed are the poor in spirit, for *theirs* is the

kingdom of heaven. Blessed are they that mourn, for they—they—"

"Sh——"

"For they—a—"

"S, H, A—"

"For they S, H—Oh, I don't know what it is!"

*"Shall!"*

"Oh, *shall!* for they shall—for they shall—a—a—shall mourn—a—a—blessed are they that shall—they that—a—they that shall mourn, for they shall—a—shall *what?* Why don't you tell me, Mary? What do you want to be so mean for?"

"Oh, Tom, you poor thickheaded thing, I'm not teasing you. I wouldn't do that. You must go and learn it again. Don't you be discouraged, Tom, you'll manage it—and if you do, I'll give you something ever so nice. There now, that's a good boy."

"All right! What is it, Mary, tell me what it is."

"Never you mind, Tom. You know if I say it's nice, it *is* nice."

"You bet you that's so, Mary. All right, I'll tackle it again."

And he did "tackle it again"—and under the double pressure of curiosity and prospective gain, he did it with such spirit that he accomplished a shining success. Mary gave him a bran-new "Barlow" knife worth twelve and a half cents; and the convulsion of delight that swept his system shook him to his foundations. True, the knife would not cut anything, but it was a "sure-enough" Barlow, and there was inconceivable grandeur in that— though where the western boys ever got the idea that such a weapon could possibly be counterfeited to its injury, is an imposing mystery and will always remain so, perhaps. Tom contrived to scarify the cupboard with it, and was arranging to begin on the bureau, when he was called off to dress for Sunday school.

Mary gave him a tin basin of water and a piece of soap, and he went outside the door and set the basin on a little bench there; then he dipped the soap in the water and laid it down; turned up his sleeves; poured out the water on the ground, gently, and then entered the kitchen and began to wipe his face diligently on the towel behind the door. But Mary removed the towel and said:

"Now ain't you ashamed, Tom. You mustn't be so bad. Water won't hurt you."

Tom was a trifle disconcerted. The basin was refilled, and this time he stood over it a little while, gathering resolution; took in a big breath and began. When he entered the kitchen presently, with both eyes shut and groping for the towel with his hands, an honorable testimony of suds and water was dripping from his face. But when he emerged from the towel, he was not yet satisfactory, for the clean territory stopped short at his chin and his jaws, like a mask; below and beyond this line there was a dark expanse of unirrigated soil that spread downward in front and backward around his neck. Mary took him by the hand, and when she was done with him he was a man and a brother, without distinction of color, and his saturated hair was neatly brushed, and its short curls wrought into a dainty and symmetrical general effect. (He privately smoothed out the curls, with labor and difficulty, and plastered his hair close down to his head; for he held curls to be effeminate, and his own filled his life with bitterness.) Then Mary got out a suit of his clothing that had been used only on Sundays during two years—they were simply called his "other clothes"—and so by that we know the size of his wardrobe. The girl "put him to rights" after he had dressed himself; she buttoned his neat roundabout up to his chin, turned his vast shirt collar down over his shoulders, brushed him off, and crowned him with his speckled straw hat. He now looked exceedingly improved and uncomfortable. He was fully as uncomfortable as he looked; for there was a restraint about whole clothes and cleanliness that galled him. He hoped that Mary would forget his shoes, but the hope was blighted; she coated them thoroughly with tallow, as was the custom, and brought them out. He lost his temper and said he was always being made to do everything he didn't want to do. But Mary said, persuasively:

"Please, Tom—that's a good boy."

So he got into the shoes snarling. Mary was soon ready, and the three children set out for Sunday school—a place that Tom hated with his whole heart; but Sid and Mary were fond of it.

Sabbath school hours were from nine to half-past ten; and then church service. Two of the children always remained for the sermon voluntarily, and the other always remained too—for stronger reasons. The church's high-backed, uncushioned pews would seat about three hundred persons; the edifice was but a small, plain affair, with a sort of pine board tree-box on top of it for a steeple. At the door Tom dropped back a step and accosted a Sunday-dressed comrade.

"Say, Billy, got a yaller ticket?"

"Yes."

"What'll you take for her?"

"What'll you give?"

"Piece of lickrish and a fishhook."

"Let's see 'em."

Tom exhibited. They were satisfactory, and the property changed hands. Then Tom traded a couple of white alleys for three red tickets, and some small trifle or other for a couple of blue ones. He waylaid other boys as they came, and went on buying tickets of various colors ten or fifteen minutes longer. He entered the church, now with a swarm of clean and noisy boys and girls, proceeded to his seat and started a quarrel with the first boy that came handy. The teacher, a grave, elderly man, interfered;

then turned his back a moment and Tom pulled a boy's hair in the next bench, and was absorbed in his book when the boy turned around; stuck a pin in another boy, presently, in order to hear him say "Ouch!" and got a new reprimand from his teacher. Tom's whole class were of a pattern—restless, noisy, and troublesome. When they came to recite their lessons, not one of them knew his verses perfectly, but had to be prompted all along. However, they worried through, and each got his reward —in small blue tickets, each with a passage of Scripture on it; each blue ticket was pay for two verses of the recitation. Ten blue tickets equaled a red one, and could be exchanged for it; ten red tickets equaled a yellow one; for ten yellow tickets the superintendent gave a very plainly bound Bible (worth forty cents in those easy times) to the pupil. How many of my readers would have the industry and application to memorize two thousand verses, even for a Doré Bible? And yet Mary had acquired two Bibles in this way—it was the patient work of two years—and a boy of German parentage had won four or five. He once recited three thousand verses without stopping; but the strain upon his mental faculties was too great, and he was little better than an idiot from that day forth—a grievous misfortune for the school, for on great occasions, before company, the superintendent (as Tom expressed it) had always made this boy come out and "spread himself." Only the older pupils managed to keep their tickets and stick to their tedious work long enough to get a Bible, and so the delivery of one of these prizes was a rare and noteworthy circumstance; the successful pupil was so great and conspicuous for that day that on the spot every scholar's heart was fired with a fresh ambition that often lasted a couple of weeks. It is possible that Tom's mental stomach had never really hungered for one of those prizes, but unquestionably his entire being had for many a day longed for the glory that came with it.

In due course the superintendent stood up in front of the pulpit, with a closed hymnbook in his hand and his forefinger inserted between its leaves, and commanded attention. When a Sunday school superintendent makes his customary little speech, a hymnbook in the hand is as necessary as is the inevitable sheet of music in the hand of a singer who stands forward on the platform and sings a solo at a concert—though why, is a mystery: for neither the hymnbook nor the sheet of music is ever referred to by the sufferer. This superintendent was a slim creature of thirty-five, with a sandy goatee and short sandy hair; he wore a stiff standing collar whose upper edge almost reached his ears and whose sharp points curved forward abreast the corners of his mouth —a fence that compelled a straight lookout ahead, and a turning of the whole body when a side view was required; his chin was propped on a spreading cravat which was as broad and as long as a banknote, and had fringed ends; his boot toes were turned sharply up, in the fashion of the day, like sleigh runners—an effect patiently and laboriously produced by the young men by

sitting with their toes pressed against a wall for hours together. Mr. Walters was very earnest of mien, and very sincere and honest at heart; and he held sacred things and places in such reverence, and so separated them from worldly matters, that unconsciously to himself his Sunday school voice had acquired a peculiar intonation which was wholly absent on weekdays. He began after this fashion:

"Now, children, I want you all to sit up just as straight and pretty as you can and give me all your attention for a minute or two. There—that is it. That is the way good little boys and girls should do. I see one little girl who is looking out of the window—I am afraid she thinks I am out there somewhere—perhaps up in one of the trees making a speech to the little birds. (Applausive titter.) I want to tell you how good it makes me feel to see so many bright, clean little faces assembled in a place like this, learning to do right and be good." And so forth and so on. It is not necessary to set down the rest of the oration. It was of a pattern which does not vary, and so it is familiar to us all.

The last third of the speech was marred by the re-
sumption of fights and other recreations among certain
of the bad boys, and by fidgetings and whisperings that
extended far and wide, washing even to the bases of
isolated and incorruptible rocks like Sid and Mary. But
now every sound ceased suddenly, with the subsidence
of Mr. Walters' voice, and the conclusion of the speech
was received with a burst of silent gratitude.

A good part of the whispering had been occasioned by
an event which was more or less rare—the entrance of
visitors: lawyer Thatcher, accompanied by a very feeble
and aged man; a fine, portly, middle-aged gentleman
with iron-gray hair; and a dignified lady who was
doubtless the latter's wife. The lady was leading a child.

Tom had been restless and full of chafings and repinings; conscience-smitten, too—he could not meet Amy Lawrence's eye, he could not brook her loving gaze. But when he saw this small newcomer his soul was all ablaze with bliss in a moment. The next moment he was "showing off" with all his might—cuffing boys, pulling hair, making faces—in a word, using every art that seemed likely to fascinate a girl and win her applause. His exaltation had but one alloy—the memory of his humiliation in this angel's garden—and that record in sand was fast washing out, under the waves of happiness that were sweeping over it now.

The visitors were given the highest seat of honor, and as soon as Mr. Walters' speech was finished, he introduced them to the school. The middle-aged man turned out to be a prodigious personage—no less a one than the county judge—altogether the most august creation these children had ever looked upon—and they wondered what kind of material he was made of—and they half wanted to hear him roar, and were half afraid he might, too. He was from Constantinople, twelve miles away—so he had traveled, and seen the world—these very eyes had looked upon the county courthouse—which was said to have a tin roof. The awe which these reflections inspired was attested by the impressive silence and the ranks of staring eyes. This was the great Judge Thatcher, brother of their own lawyer. Jeff Thatcher immediately went forward, to be familiar with the great man and be envied by the school. It would have been music to his soul to hear the whisperings:

"Look at him, Jim! He's a-going up there. Say—look! he's a-going to shake hands with him—he *is* shaking hands with him! By jings, don't you wish you was Jeff?"

Mr. Walters fell to "showing off," with all sorts of official bustlings and activities, giving orders, delivering judgments, discharging directions here, there, everywhere that he could find a target. The librarian "showed off"—running hither and thither with his arms full of books and making a deal of the splutter and fuss that insect authority delights in. The young lady teachers "showed off"—bending sweetly over pupils that were lately being boxed, lifting pretty warning fingers at bad little boys and patting good ones lovingly. The young gentlemen teachers "showed off" with small scoldings and other little displays of authority and fine attention to discipline—and most of the teachers, of both sexes, found business up at the library, by the pulpit; and it was business that frequently had to be done over again two or three times (with much seeming vexation). The little girls "showed off" in various ways, and the little boys "showed off" with such diligence that the air was thick with paper wads and the murmur of scufflings. And above it all the great man sat and beamed a majestic judicial smile upon all the house, and warmed himself in the sun of his own grandeur—for he was "showing off," too.

There was only one thing wanting to make Mr. Walters' ecstasy complete, and that was a chance to deliver a Bible prize and exhibit a prodigy. Several pupils had a few yellow tickets, but none had enough—he had been around among the star pupils inquiring. He would have given worlds, now, to have that German lad back again with a sound mind.

And now at this moment, when hope was dead, Tom Sawyer came forward with nine yellow tickets, nine red tickets, and ten blue ones, and demanded a Bible. This was a thunderbolt out of a clear sky. Walters was not expecting an application from this source for the next ten years. But there was no getting around it—here were the certified checks, and they were good for their face. Tom was therefore elevated to a place with the Judge and the other elect, and the great news was announced from headquarters. It was the most stunning surprise of the decade, and so profound was the sensation that it lifted the new hero up to the judicial one's altitude, and the school had two marvels to gaze upon in place of one. The boys were all eaten up with envy—but those that suffered the bitterest pangs were those who perceived too late that they themselves had contributed to this hated splendor by trading tickets to Tom for the wealth he had amassed in selling white-washing privileges. These despised themselves, as being the dupes of a wily fraud, a guileful snake in the grass.

The prize was delivered to Tom with as much effusion as the superintendent could pump up under the circumstances; but it lacked somewhat of the true gush, for the poor fellow's instinct taught him that there was a mystery here that could not well bear the light, perhaps; it was simply preposterous that *this* boy had warehoused two thousand sheaves of Scriptural wisdom on his premises—a dozen would strain his capacity, without a doubt.

Amy Lawrence was proud and glad, and she tried to make Tom see it in her face—but he wouldn't look. She

wondered; then she was just a grain troubled; next a dim
suspicion came and went—came again; she watched; a
furtive glance told her worlds—and then her heart
broke, and she was jealous, and angry, and the tears
came and she hated everybody. Tom most of all (she
thought).

Tom was introduced to the Judge; but his tongue was
tied, his breath would hardly come, his heart quaked—
partly because of the awful greatness of the man, but
mainly because he was *her* parent. He would have liked
to fall down and worship him, if it were in the dark. The
Judge put his hand on Tom's head and called him a fine
little man, and asked him what his name was. The boy
stammered, gasped, and got it out:

"Tom."

"Oh, no, not Tom—it is—"

"Thomas."

"Ah, that's it. I thought there was more to it, maybe. That's very well. But you've another one I daresay, and you'll tell it to me, won't you?"

"Tell the gentleman your other name, Thomas," said Walters, "and say *sir.* You mustn't forget your manners."

"Thomas Sawyer—sir."

"That's it! That's a good boy. Fine boy. Fine, manly little fellow. Two thousand verses is a great many—very, very great many. And you never can be sorry for the trouble you took to learn them; for knowledge is worth more than anything there is in the world; it's what makes great men and good men; you'll be a great man and a good man yourself, some day, Thomas, and then you'll look back and say, 'It's all owing to the precious Sunday school privileges of my boyhood—it's all owing to my dear teachers that taught me to learn—it's all owing to the good superintendent, who encouraged me, and watched over me, and gave me a beautiful Bible—a splendid elegant Bible—to keep and have it all for my own, always—it's all owing to right bringing up!' That is what you will say, Thomas—and you wouldn't take any money for those two thousand verses—no indeed you wouldn't. And now you wouldn't mind telling me and this lady some of the things you've learned—no, I know you wouldn't—for we are proud of little boys that learn. Now, no doubt you know the names of all the twelve disciples. Won't you tell us the names of the first two that were appointed?"

Tom was tugging at a buttonhole and looking sheepish. He blushed, now, and his eyes fell. Mr. Walters' heart sank within him. He said to himself, "It is not possible that the boy can answer the simplest question—why *did* the Judge ask him?" Yet he felt obliged to speak up and say:

"Answer the gentleman, Thomas—don't be afraid."

Tom still hung fire.

"Now I know you'll tell *me*," said the lady. "The names of the first two disciples were—"

"DAVID AND GOLIATH!"

Let us draw the curtain of charity over the rest of the scene.

# Amelia Bedelia

**by Peggy Parish**
**Illustrated by Fritz Siebel**

*On the new maid's first day at work, Mr. and Mrs. Rogers have to be away from home. They leave a list of things to do, but what they don't know is that Amelia Bedelia has her own idea of how to follow directions. Wait until they see!*

"Oh, Amelia Bedelia, your first day of work. And I can't be here. But I made a list for you. You do just what the list says," said Mrs. Rogers. Mrs. Rogers got into the car with Mr. Rogers. They drove away.

"My, what nice folks. I'm going to like working here," said Amelia Bedelia.

Amelia Bedelia went inside. "Such a grand house. These must be rich folks. But I must get to work. Here I stand just looking. And me with a whole list of things to do."

Amelia Bedelia stood there a minute longer. "I think I'll make a surprise for them. I'll make a lemon-meringue pie. I do make good pies."

So Amelia Bedelia went into the kitchen. She put a little of this and a pinch of that into a bowl. She mixed and she rolled. Soon her pie was ready to go into the oven.

"There," said Amelia Bedelia. "That's done. Now let's see what this list says."

Amelia Bedelia read,

# CHANGE THE TOWELS IN THE GREEN BATHROOM.

Amelia Bedelia found the green bathroom.

"Those towels are very nice. Why change them?" she thought. Then Amelia Bedelia remembered what Mrs. Rogers had said. She must do just what the list told her.

"Well, all right," said Amelia Bedelia.

Amelia Bedelia got some scissors. She snipped a little here and a little there. And she changed those towels.

"There," said Amelia Bedelia. She looked at her list
again.

# DUST THE FURNITURE.

"Did you ever hear tell of such a silly thing? At my
house we undust the furniture. But to each his own
way."

Amelia Bedelia took one last look at the bathroom.
She saw a big box with the words *Dusting Powder* on it.

"Well, look at that. A special powder to dust with!"
exclaimed Amelia Bedelia.

So Amelia Bedelia dusted the furniture.

"That should be dusty enough. My, how nice it
smells."

# DRAW THE DRAPES WHEN THE SUN COMES IN.

read Amelia Bedelia. She looked up. The sun was coming in. Amelia Bedelia looked at the list again.

"Draw the drapes? That's what it says. I'm not much of a hand at drawing, but I'll try."

So Amelia Bedelia sat right down and she drew those drapes. Amelia Bedelia marked off about the drapes.

"Now what?"

# PUT THE LIGHTS OUT WHEN YOU FINISH IN THE LIVING ROOM.

Amelia Bedelia thought about this a minute. She switched off the lights. Then she carefully unscrewed each bulb. And Amelia Bedelia put the lights out.

"So those things need to be aired out, too. Just like pillows and babies. Oh, I do have a lot to learn.

"My pie!" exclaimed Amelia Bedelia. She hurried to the kitchen.

"Just right," she said. She took the pie out of the oven and put it on the table to cool. Then she looked at the list.

# MEASURE TWO CUPS OF RICE.

"That's next," said Amelia Bedelia. Amelia Bedelia found two cups. She filled them with rice. And Amelia Bedelia measured that rice.

Amelia Bedelia laughed. "These folks do want me to do funny things." Then she poured the rice back into the container.

THE MEAT MARKET WILL DELIVER
A STEAK AND A CHICKEN.
PLEASE TRIM THE FAT BEFORE
YOU PUT THE STEAK IN THE
ICEBOX.
AND PLEASE DRESS THE CHICKEN.

When the meat arrived, Amelia Bedelia opened the bag. She looked at the steak for a long time.

"Yes," she said. "That will do nicely." Amelia Bedelia got some lace and bits of ribbon. And Amelia Bedelia trimmed that fat before she put the steak in the icebox.

"Now I must dress the chicken. I wonder if she wants a he chicken or a she chicken?" said Amelia Bedelia.

Amelia Bedelia went right to work. Soon the chicken was finished. Amelia Bedelia heard the door open.

"The folks are back," she said. She rushed out to meet them.

"Amelia Bedelia, why are all the light bulbs outside?" asked Mr. Rogers.

"The list just said to put the lights out," said Amelia Bedelia. "It didn't say to bring them back in. Oh, I do hope they didn't get aired too long."

"Amelia Bedelia, the sun will fade the furniture. I asked you to draw the drapes," said Mrs. Rogers.

"I did! I did! See," said Amelia Bedelia. She held up her picture.

Then Mrs. Rogers saw the furniture. "The furniture!" she cried.

"Did I dust it well enough?" asked Amelia Bedelia. "That's such nice dusting powder."

Mr. Rogers went to wash his hands. "I say," he called. "These are very unusual towels."

Mrs. Rogers dashed into the bathroom. "Oh, my best towels," she said.

"Didn't I change them enough?" asked Amelia Bedelia.

Mrs. Rogers went to the kitchen. "I'll cook the dinner. Where is the rice I asked you to measure?"

"I put it back in the container. But I remember—it measured four and a half inches," said Amelia Bedelia.

"Was the meat delivered?" asked Mrs. Rogers.

"Yes," said Amelia Bedelia. "I trimmed the fat just like you said. It does look nice."

Mrs. Rogers rushed to the icebox. She opened it.

"Lace! Ribbons! Oh, dear!" said Mrs. Rogers.

"The chicken—you dressed the chicken?" asked Mrs. Rogers.

"Yes, and I found the nicest box to put him in," said Amelia Bedelia.

"Box!" exclaimed Mrs. Rogers.

Mrs. Rogers hurried over to the box. She lifted the lid. There lay the chicken. And he was just as dressed as he could be.

Mrs. Rogers was angry. She was very angry. She opened her mouth. Mrs. Rogers meant to tell Amelia Bedelia she was fired. But before she could get the words out, Mr. Rogers put something in her mouth. It was so good Mrs. Rogers forgot about being angry.

"Lemon-meringue pie!" she exclaimed.

"I made it to surprise you," said Amelia Bedelia happily. So right then and there Mr. and Mrs. Rogers decided that Amelia Bedelia must stay. And so she did.

Mrs. Rogers learned to say undust the furniture, un-light the lights, close the drapes, and things like that. Mr. Rogers didn't care if Amelia Bedelia trimmed all of his steaks with lace.

All he cared about was having her there to make lemon-meringue pie.

# Apples and Mrs. Stetson

by Robert Newton Peck

*When your best friend is a boy named Soup, you get into more trouble than usual. Especially when you start "whipping" little green apples —hard little green apples—in the vicinity of certain windows.*

Soup was my best pal.

His real and righteous name was Luther Wesley Vinson, but nobody called him Luther. He didn't like it. I called him Luther just once, which prompted Soup to break me of a very bad habit before it really got formed. As soon as the swelling went out of my lip, I called him Soup instead of Thoop.

He first discouraged his mother of the practice of calling him Luther. (Using a different method, of course.) She used to call him home to mealtime by yelling, "Luther!" But he never answered to the name. He'd rather miss supper. When his mother got wise, she'd stand out on their back porch, cup her hands to her mouth, and yell, "Soup's on!"

From a distance (their farm was uproad next to ours) all you could hear was "Soup." And that was how the kids who were playing ball in the pasture started thinking his name was Soup, because he answered to it.

When it came to getting the two of us in trouble, Soup was a regular genius. He liked to whip apples. But that was nothing new. Every kid did. The apples had to be small and green and hard, about the size of a golf ball.

The whip had to be about four to five foot long, with a point on the small end that you'd whittle sharp with your jackknife. You held the apple close to your chest with your left hand and pushed the pointed stick into the apple, but not so far as it'd come out the yonder side. No matter how careful you speared the apple, a few drops of juice would squirt on your shirt. They dried to small, tiny brown spots that never even came out in the wash.

Sassafras made the best whips. You could swing a sassafras whip through the air so fast it would whistle. The apple would fly off, and you'd think it would never come down. To whip an apple was sport enough for most of us, but not for old Soup.

"Watch this," he said.

"What?" I said.

We were up in the apple orchard on a hillside that overlooked town. Below us was the Baptist church.

"I bet I can hit the Baptist church."

"You better not, Soup."

"Why not?"

"We'll really catch it."

"No we won't. And what's more, I bet this apple can hit the bell in the belltower and make it ring."

"Aw, it won't go that far."

"Oh, no?"

Soup whipped his apple, and I was right. It landed far short of the Baptist church.

"Watch me," I said. And with my next throw I almost hit the church roof.

"My turn," said Soup.

I'll have to admit that Soup put all he had into his next throw. The whip made a whistle that would've called a dead dog. That old apple took off like it'd been shot out of a gun, made a big arc through the sky, and for a few long seconds I thought we'd hear that old bell ring for sure.

But we never heard the sounding brass. What we heard was the tinkling cymbal of a broken window. Breaking a pane of plain old glass wasn't stylish enough for Soup. It had to be stained glass. Even the sound of that stained glass shattering had color in it. I just stood there looking at that tiny little black star of emptiness that was once a window pane. It was like somebody busted my heart.

"No," I said, in almost a whisper.

I wanted the glass to fly up into place again, like it never happened. So that the little black star would erase away like a bad dream. But there it was and there it stayed.

"No," said Soup.

My feet were stuck to the ground like I was standing in twin buckets of mortar. I couldn't run. Not even when a lady ran out of the side door of the church and pointed up at us. Even though she was far below, it felt like her finger took a stab right into my chest. It was a pain, just like when you get stuck with the tip of a sword.

To make matters worse, it was Mrs. Stetson.

My family wasn't Baptist. But I guess that she knew Mama and Aunt Carrie real well, because she came to call almost every week. Religion was her favorite subject. You'd be hard put to find a soul who knew more about God than Mrs. Stetson. She was a walking, talking Bible, which she could quote chapter and verse. Get her started and it went on like rain. Forty days and forty nights. Just to be in the same room with Mrs. Stetson was like being caught in a downpour. She sure could drench a body with scripture.

But what she was saying now was far from holy. And if there was anything Mrs. Stetson was poor at, it was talking as she climbed full-speed up a steep hill. By the time she reached me, she was so out of breath from the uphill scolding that she couldn't say a word.

I looked around for Soup, but he was gone. Good old Soup. So there I stood, with a sassafras stick in my hand and apple-juice spots on the front of my shirt. Still wet. The mortar in my shoes had now hardened into stone. My ears were ringing with a *tinkle tinkle tinkle* of smashing glass that wouldn't seem to stop.

"You!" she said.

"Me?"

Her eyes burned with the wrath of the Old Testament. It was plain to behold that Mrs. Stetson believed that

you had to smite transgressors so that the ground ran red with their blood until the multitudes were sore afraid. Especially sore. But if anybody ever looked sore, it was Mrs. Stetson.

"Robert Peck!" she said in full voice.

Her big old hands shot out and grabbed my face and my hair. She shook me hard enough to shake off one of my shoes. Then after she stopped shaking me, she twisted my head around so my nose was pointing right at the little black star of that broken window pane.

"Just look what you did!" said Mrs. Stetson. "Look me in the eye and tell the truth. Do you dare say you didn't?"

"I didn't."

This was not the response that she expected. I guess what she really sought was an outburst of guilt, a tear-soaked plea to ask for the forgiveness of God and Mrs. Stetson—perhaps not in that order of importance.

"I didn't. Honest, Mrs. Stetson. I didn't throw an apple that far. Look how far it is."

"You *did* do it. I saw you do it. And here's the apple you did it with." She had a pierced apple in one hand and my switch in the other, and I knew I was a goner.

"But I couldn't hit the church from way up here. Nobody could."

"Bosh! Even a fool knows how far an apple will pitch from a stick. Watch."

You won't believe what I saw. Mrs. Stetson somehow let go of her senses. She pushed an apple on a stick, and before I could grab her arm, her temper bested reason. Whissshh! You never saw a worse throw in your life, not if you stood up in that old orchard from now until Judgment. Her apple never even headed in the direction of the Baptist church. Nowhere near. But you couldn't say that apple didn't have any steam to it. No, sir. It flew off her stick (my stick) like a rifle ball, going east by northeast, and finally tipped over a flower pot with a geranium in it outside old Haskin's shack window. And the pot cracked the glass.

Crash-tinkle!

Out came old Mr. Haskin with blood in his eye. His language would have made Satan himself cover his ears. Not real fancy swearing, just a long string of old favorites. He pointed at Mrs. Stetson and me, then he started uphill and coming our way fast.

"Run!" yelled Mrs. Stetson. "That man's a degenerate."

We ran, Mrs. Stetson and I. She had on two shoes and I wore one, which evened the speed a bit, and we ran as if Hell was a step behind. We ran until we could no longer hear the terrible things that old Haskin shouted he would do to Mrs. Stetson the next time she came near his rotten old shack. We didn't stop running, Mrs. Stetson and I, until we darted into Frank Rooker's garage and had bolted the door.

But as we ran in, Soup ran out, after taking one look at Mrs. Stetson. Out the side door he shot, into the arms of Mr. Haskin. Soup still had his switch in hand, and his shirt-front was smelled and spotted with apple juice, which was enough evidence for old Haskin. Borrowing the sassafras switch, the old man gave Soup a fine smarting. I'll have to admit it sure must have been a sight to see.

From where Mrs. Stetson and I stood panting, we didn't see it. But we heard it all. Thinking I'd be next, I even winced for poor Soup with every blow. Best of all, we heard him confess up to breaking the window, even though it wasn't the same glass he got thrashed for. In a way, it really was justice.

Mrs. Stetson was right. There really is a God.

# Pippi Goes to School
## by Astrid Lindgren

*What is it like to have a neighbor who is nine years old, lives in a house all by herself, has her own monkey and her own horse, and never has to go to school? Meet Pippi Longstocking and find out.*

Of course Tommy and Annika went to school. Each morning at eight o'clock they trotted off, hand in hand, swinging their schoolbags.

At that time Pippi was usually grooming her horse or dressing Mr. Nilsson, her monkey, in his little suit. Or else she was taking her morning exercises, which meant turning forty-three somersaults in a row. Then she would sit down on the kitchen table and, utterly happy, drink a large cup of coffee and eat a piece of bread and cheese.

Tommy and Annika always looked longingly toward Villa Villekulla as they started off to school. They would much rather have gone to play with Pippi. If only Pippi had been going to school too; that would have been something else again.

"Just think what fun we could have on the way home from school," said Tommy.

"Yes, and on the way to school too," said Annika.

The more they thought about it the worse they felt to think that Pippi did not go to school, and at last they determined to try to persuade her to begin.

"You can't imagine what a nice teacher we have," said Tommy artfully to Pippi one afternoon when he and Annika had come for a visit at Villa Villekulla after they had finished their homework.

"If you only knew what fun it is in school!" Annika added. "I'd die if I couldn't go to school."

Pippi sat on a hassock, bathing her feet in a tub. She said nothing but just wiggled her toes for a while so that the water splashed around everywhere.

"You don't have to stay so very long," continued Tommy. "Just until two o'clock."

"Yes, and besides, we get Christmas vacation and Easter vacation and summer vacation," said Annika.

Pippi bit her big toe thoughtfully but still said nothing. Suddenly, as if she had made some decision, she poured all the water out on the kitchen floor, so that Mr. Nilsson, who sat near her playing with a mirror, got his pants absolutely soaked.

"It's not fair!" said Pippi sternly without paying any attention to Mr. Nilsson's puzzled air about his wet pants. "It is absolutely unfair! I don't intend to stand it!"

"What's the matter now?" asked Tommy.

"In four months it will be Christmas, and then you'll have Christmas vacation. But I, what'll I get?" Pippi's voice sounded sad. "No Christmas vacation, not even the tiniest bit of a Christmas vacation," she complained. "Something will have to be done about that. Tomorrow morning I'll begin school."

Tommy and Annika clapped their hands with delight. "Hurrah! We'll wait for you outside our gate at eight o'clock."

"Oh, no," said Pippi. "I can't begin as early as that. And besides, I'm going to ride to school."

And ride she did. Exactly at ten o'clock the next day she lifted her horse off the porch, and a little later all the people in the town ran to their windows to see what horse it was that was running away. That is to say, they thought he was running away, but it was only Pippi in a bit of a hurry to get to school.

She galloped wildly into the schoolyard, jumped off the horse, tied him to a tree, and burst into the schoolroom with such a noise and a clatter that Tommy and Annika and all their classmates jumped in their seats.

"Hi, there," cried Pippi, waving her big hat. "Did I get here in time for pluttifikation?"

Tommy and Annika had told their teacher that a new girl named Pippi Longstocking was coming, and the teacher had already heard about Pippi in the little town. As she was a very pleasant teacher, she had decided to do all she could to make Pippi happy in school.

Pippi threw herself down on a vacant bench without having been invited to do so, but the teacher paid no attention to her heedless way. She simply said in a very friendly voice, "Welcome to school, little Pippi. I hope that you will enjoy yourself here and learn a great deal."

"Yes, and I hope I'll get some Christmas vacation," said Pippi. "That is the reason I've come. It's only fair, you know."

"If you would first tell me your whole name," said the teacher, "then I'll register you in school."

"My name is Pippilotta Delicatessa Windowshade Mackrelmint Efraim's Daughter Longstocking, daughter of Captain Efraim Longstocking, formerly the Terror of the Sea, now a cannibal king. Pippi is really only a nickname, because Papa thought that Pippilotta was too long to say."

"Indeed?" said the teacher. "Well, then we shall call you Pippi too. But now," she continued, "suppose we test you a little and see what you know. You are a big girl and no doubt know a great deal already. Let us begin with arithmetic. Pippi, can you tell me what seven and five are?"

Pippi, astonished and dismayed, looked at her and said, "Well, if you don't know that yourself, you needn't think I'm going to tell you."

All the children stared in horror at Pippi, and the teacher explained that one couldn't answer that way in school.

"I beg your pardon," said Pippi contritely. "I didn't know that. I won't do it again."

"No, let us hope not," said the teacher. "And now I will tell you that seven and five are twelve."

"See that!" said Pippi. "You knew it yourself. Why are you asking then?"

The teacher decided to act as if nothing unusual were happening and went on with her examination.

"Well now, Pippi, how much do you think eight and four are?"

"Oh, about sixty-seven," hazarded Pippi.

"Of course not," said the teacher. "Eight and four are twelve."

"Well now, really, my dear little woman," said Pippi, "that is carrying things too far. You just said that seven and five are twelve. There should be some rhyme and reason to things even in school. Furthermore, if you are so childishly interested in that foolishness, why don't you sit down in a corner by yourself and do arithmetic and leave us alone so we can play tag?"

The teacher decided there was no point in trying to teach Pippi any more arithmetic. She began to ask the other children the arithmetic questions.

"Can Tommy answer this one?" she asked. "If Lisa has seven apples and Axel has nine apples, how many apples do they have together?"

"Yes, you tell, Tommy," Pippi interrupted, "and tell me too, if Lisa gets a stomach-ache and Axel gets more stomach-ache, whose fault is it and where did they get hold of the apples in the first place?"

The teacher tried to pretend that she hadn't heard and turned to Annika. "Now, Annika, here's an example for you: Gustav was with his schoolmates on a picnic. He had a quarter when he started out and seven cents when he got home. How much did he spend?"

"Yes, indeed," said Pippi, "and I also want to know why he was so extravagant, and if it was pop he bought, and if he washed his ears properly before he left home."

The teacher decided to give up arithmetic altogether. She thought maybe Pippi would prefer to learn to read. So she took out a pretty little card with a picture of an ibex on it. In front of the ibex's nose was the letter *i*.

"Now, Pippi," she said briskly, "you'll see something jolly. You see here an ibex. And the letter in front of this ibex is called *i.*"

"That I'll never believe," said Pippi. "I think it looks exactly like a straight line with a little fly speck over it. But what I'd really like to know is, what has the ibex to do with the fly speck?"

The teacher took out another card with a picture of a snake on it and told Pippi that the letter on that was an *s.*

"Speaking of snakes," said Pippi, "I'll never, ever forget the time I had a fight with a huge snake in India. You can't imagine what a dreadful snake it was, fourteen yards long and mad as a hornet, and every day he ate up five Indians and then two little children for dessert, and one time he came and wanted me for dessert, and he wound himself around me—uhhh!—but I've been around a bit, I said, and hit him in the head, bang, and then he hissed *uiuiuiuiuiuiuiuitch,* and then I hit him again, and bingo! he was dead, and, indeed, so that is the letter *s*—most remarkable!"

Pippi had to stop to get her breath. And the teacher, who had now begun to think that Pippi was an unruly and troublesome child, decided that the class should have drawing for a while. Surely Pippi could sit still and be quiet and draw, thought the teacher. She took out paper and pencils and passed them out to the children.

"Now you may draw whatever you wish," she said and sat down at her desk and began to correct homework. In a little while she looked up to see how the drawing was going. All the children sat looking at Pippi, who lay flat on the floor, drawing to her heart's content.

"But, Pippi," said the teacher impatiently, "why in the world aren't you drawing on your paper?"

"I filled that long ago. There isn't room enough for my whole horse on that little snip of paper," said Pippi. "Just now I'm working on his front legs, but when I get to his tail I guess I'll have to go out in the hall."

The teacher thought hard for a while. "Suppose instead we all sing a little song," she suggested.

All the children stood up by their seats except Pippi; she stayed where she was on the floor. "You go ahead and sing," she said. "I'll rest myself a while. Too much learning breaks even the healthiest."

But now the teacher's patience came to an end. She told all the children to go out into the yard so she could talk to Pippi alone.

When the teacher and Pippi were alone, Pippi got up and walked to the desk. "Do you know what?" she said. "It was awfully jolly to come to school to find out what it was like. But I don't think I care about going to school any more, Christmas vacation or no Christmas vacation. There's altogether too many apples and ibexes and snakes and things like that. It makes me dizzy in the head. I hope that you, Teacher, won't be sorry."

But the teacher said she certainly was sorry, most of all because Pippi wouldn't behave decently; and that any girl who acted as badly as Pippi did wouldn't be allowed to go to school even if she wanted to ever so.

"Have I behaved badly?" asked Pippi, much astonished. "Goodness, I didn't know that," she added and looked very sad. And nobody could look as sad as Pippi when she was sad. She stood silent for a while, and then she said in a trembling voice, "You understand, Teacher, don't you, that when you have a mother who's an angel and a father who is a cannibal king, and when you have sailed on the ocean all your whole life, then you don't know just how to behave in school with all the apples and ibexes."

Then the teacher said she understood and didn't feel annoyed with Pippi any longer, and maybe Pippi could come back to school when she was a little older. Pippi positively beamed with delight. "I think you are awfully nice, Teacher. And here is something for you."

Out of her pocket Pippi took a lovely little gold watch and laid it on the desk. The teacher said she couldn't possibly accept such a valuable gift from Pippi, but Pippi replied, "You've got to take it; otherwise I'll come back again tomorrow, and that would be a pretty how-do-you-do."

Then Pippi rushed out to the schoolyard and jumped on her horse. All the children gathered around to pat the horse and see her off.

"You ought to know about the schools in Argentina," said Pippi, looking down at the children. "That's where you should go. Easter vacation begins three days after Christmas vacation ends, and when Easter vacation is over there are three days and then it's summer vacation. Summer vacation ends on the first of November, and then you have a tough time until Christmas vacation begins on November 11. But you can stand that because there are at least no lessons. It is strictly against the law to have lessons in Argentina. Once in a while it happens that some Argentine kid sneaks into a closet and sits there studying a lesson, but it's just too bad for him if his mother finds him. Arithmetic they don't have at all in the schools, and if there is any kid who knows what seven and five are he has to stand in the corner all day— that is, if he's foolish enough to let the teacher know that he knows. They have reading on Friday, and then only if they have some books, which they never have."

"But what do they do in school?" asked one little boy.

"Eat caramels," said Pippi decidedly. "There is a long pipe that goes from a caramel factory nearby directly into the schoolroom, and caramels keep shooting out of it all day long so the children have all they can do to eat them up."

"Yes, but what does the teacher do?" asked one little girl.

"Takes the paper off the caramels for the children, of course," said Pippi. "You didn't suppose they did it themselves, did you? Hardly. They don't even go to school themselves—they send their brothers." Pippi waved her big hat.

"So long, kids," she cried gaily. "Now you won't see me for a while. But always remember how many apples Axel had or you'll be sorry."

With a ringing laugh Pippi rode out through the gate so wildly that the pebbles whirled around the horse's hoofs and the windowpanes rattled in the schoolhouse.

# The Boy Who Turned into a TV Set

## by Stephen Manes

*Ogden Pettibone watched television so much that one day he woke up and found that he had turned into one. He had no control over the programming, so he never knew what would come out of his mouth. As you'll see, this can be a problem on a crowded bus . . .*

The new television did not sleep well that night. The glow from his screen didn't shine through the covers, but his mouth occasionally fell open as he dozed off, and then a loud commercial or an audience howling at a comedian's joke would waken him.

He was tired and hungry when he came down to breakfast, but his parents asked him not to eat until the commercials came on so that they wouldn't miss any of the morning news. Ogden obliged them, but he did feel rather chilly sitting at the table without a shirt on.

After breakfast, he and his father rode to the doctor's office on a bus. It was crowded, but they found two seats together, and everything was fine until Ogden yawned.

"I hate to be the one to tell you this," a girl's voice said through his mouth, "but you have bad breath."

"WHAT?" stormed the enormous woman beside him. "Who said that?"

"Bad breath," the voice repeated before Ogden could close his jaws.

"I do *not!*" the woman huffed. "I don't know who you think you are, but you had better apologize, sonny!"

Ogden would have liked to, but he knew there was no telling what might come out if he opened his mouth again. He kept it shut.

"Please excuse him," his father told the woman. "I'm sure he didn't mean it."

"Then why did he say it? The least he can do is apologize for himself."

"He really is sorry," said Mr. Pettibone. "Aren't you, Ogden?"

Ogden nodded.

"You didn't mean it, did you?"

Ogden shook his head.

"Humph," the woman sniffed, and turned away.

Just then the bus went over a bump in the road, jolting its passengers so violently that Ogden's jaw dropped open again. "Do you have trouble losing weight?" asked an announcer's voice before Ogden could get himself under control.

The huge woman turned bright red and looked as though she might explode any second. Mr. Pettibone whisked his son to the exit, and marched him off the bus.

"I know it wasn't your fault," Mr. Pettibone told Ogden as they walked toward the doctor's office, "but please try to keep your mouth closed. We wouldn't want another unpleasant incident."

Ogden nodded and clenched his teeth.

The doctor's waiting room was filled with sick kids and their parents. Ogden found a book on airplanes and sat down beside his father to read it.

"My name's Jennifer," said a runny-nosed little girl who came up to him. "What's yours?"

Ogden didn't want to be unfriendly, but he thought he'd better not try to say anything.

"Hey! I said what's your name!"

Ogden just smiled, keeping his lips tight.

"Tell me your name!" the girl insisted, jumping in the air and landing right on Ogden's toes.

Ogden opened his mouth to say "Ow!" but what came out instead was a lionlike roar: "GRRRRRRRRRR!" It sounded so realistic, it scared little Jennifer back to her mother.

"Quite a cough your son has," commented the woman sitting next to Ogden's father. "I certainly hope it isn't contagious." Mr. Pettibone shook his head.

The nurse led Ogden and his father to an examining room. "The doctor will be with you shortly," she told Ogden. "Please take off all your clothes except your underpants."

Ogden did. He checked his screen. It was showing a soap opera, so he didn't bother to open his mouth to listen.

"Hello, Ogden," Doctor Stark said cheerfully when he came in a few minutes later. "What seems to be the trouble?"

Ogden pointed to the picture on his stomach. His father explained the problem.

"Hmmmm," said the doctor, bending over to take a look. "Unusual." He pointed a tongue depressor toward Ogden's mouth. "Say 'ah.'"

Ogden tried. What came out instead was a woman's voice saying, "I'm afraid there's not much hope for Penny after that terrible auto accident."

"Hmmmm," said the doctor again, and peered intently at Ogden's screen.

"Do you think it's serious?" his father asked.

"Oh, Penny will pull through," Doctor Stark reassured him. "She has to. She's the star of the show."

"But what about Ogden?" Mr. Pettibone wondered.

"Hmmmm," said Doctor Stark. He put his stethoscope in his ears and listened to his patient's chest, stomach, back, and neck. He examined Ogden's eyes and ears. Then he stuck a thermometer in Ogden's mouth and watched the soap opera for three minutes, even though he couldn't hear what the actors were saying, since Ogden had to keep his mouth closed. Finally Doctor Stark took the thermometer out again.

"No fever," he said. "Ogden, I'm afraid there's nothing I can do for you."

"But he can't even speak for himself," Mr. Pettibone protested. "Is it something like laryngitis?"

"It's a much more difficult case than that, I'm afraid. Ogden has televisionosis."

"Televisionosis?" Ogden wanted to ask. Mr. Pettibone asked it for him.

"Yes," Doctor Stark replied. "It's a disease so rare it's practically unheard of. I've certainly never heard of it before. One of my patients used to get radio stations on his tooth fillings, but this is much more severe. Your boy is exhibiting all the symptoms of a television set."

"But he doesn't want to be a television set."

"I'm afraid he has no choice. There's no known cure for televisionosis."

"Oh, my," said Mr. Pettibone, too stunned to say anything else.

"Perhaps he'll outgrow it," said the doctor pleasantly. "And if he doesn't, he'll be very popular. Everybody loves television."

# Anansi and His Visitor, Turtle

## by Edna Mason Kaula

*Tired and hungry, Turtle knocks on Anansi the Spider's door, hoping to share his meal. It's an unwritten law in Anansi's country to offer hospitality to strangers, but selfish Anansi thinks of a clever way to keep his dinner for himself.*

It was almost time for Sun to sink to his resting place when Turtle, tired and dusty from hours of wandering, came to Anansi's house in the middle of a clearing in the woods. Turtle was hungry and the appetizing aroma of freshly cooked fish and yams drew him to approach Anansi's door and to knock. Anansi jerked the door open. When he saw the tired stranger he was inwardly annoyed, but it was an unwritten law of his country that one must never, no never, refuse hospitality to a passer-by.

Anansi smiled grimly and said, "Come in, come in, and share my dinner, Mr. Turtle."

As Turtle stretched out one paw to help himself from the steaming platter Anansi almost choked on a mouthful of food. In a shocked voice he said, "Turtle, I must remind you that in my country it is ill-mannered to come to the table without first washing. Please go to the stream at the foot of the hill and wash your dusty paws."

Turtle waddled down the hill and waded in the water for a while. He even washed his face. By the time he had trudged back up the trail to Anansi's house, the platter of fish was half empty. Anansi was eating at a furious rate.

Turtle stretched out one paw to help himself to food, but again Anansi stopped him. "Turtle, your paws are still dusty. Please go wash them."

"It is the dust from the long trail up the hill," Turtle explained in a meek voice. Clearly, it was not Turtle's place to argue if he expected to share the delectable meal, so he crawled down the hill a second time and rewashed his paws. Turtle was careful to walk on the grass beside the dusty trail on the climb back to Anansi's house. He hurried, for by now he was ravenous.

But, oh dear! Anansi had scraped the platter bare of fish and yams. "My, that was a good dinner," he said, wiping the last drop of gravy from his chin.

"Thank you for your wonderful hospitality, Anansi. Someday you must visit me." And Turtle, in a huff, went on home.

Some months later Anansi visited Turtle. After creepy crawling all day from one tall grass stem to the next he found Turtle snoozing beside the river.

"Well, well," exclaimed Turtle. "So you have come to share my dinner. Make yourself comfortable, my dear Anansi, while I go below and prepare the food." He plunged into the river with a splash. Anansi was hungry. He paced the shoreline and watched for Turtle's reappearance.

At last Turtle's head popped above the water. "Dinner is ready," he called as he bit into a huge clam. "Come on down." Then he disappeared from sight.

Anansi dived head first into the water, sank a few inches, then floated to the surface. His spindly legs and tiny body prevented him from sinking. He flipped and flapped his puny arms, tried swallow dives and belly flops, but he could not reach the bed of the river.

Then that cunning spider schemed. He filled the pockets of his jacket with small round pebbles, dived into the river, and sank with a bump that landed him right at the dinner table. Before him was spread the most delicious meal he had ever seen. There were oysters and clams, mussels, slices of eel, and crabs. As a centerpiece, sprays of watercress rested against large pink shrimp. Anansi's eyes widened with pleasure, his stomach rumbled in anticipation.

Turtle, already seated at the table, swallowed a piece of eel, looked at Anansi and said, "Oh, Anansi, I must

remind you that in my country it is ill-mannered to
come to the table wearing a jacket. Please take it off."

Very slowly Anansi removed his jacket. Very slowly
Anansi left the table. Without the weight of the pebbles
to hold him down he floated straight up through the
green water and out of sight.

When you set out to outsmart another person to your
own advantage, there is usually someone who can outsmart you.

# Laughing Gas

by P. L. Travers
Illustrated by Mary Shepard

*Mary Poppins is a typical English nursemaid: prim, proper, and very strict with children. But strange and magical things seem to happen when Mary Poppins is around, as Jane and Michael find out when they go on a visit to Mary's uncle, Mr. Wigg.*

"Are you quite sure he will be at home?" said Jane, as they got off the Bus, she and Michael and Mary Poppins.

"Would my Uncle ask me to bring you to tea if he intended to go out, I'd like to know?" said Mary Poppins, who was evidently very offended by the question. She was wearing her blue coat with the silver buttons and the blue hat to match, and on the days when she wore these it was the easiest thing in the world to offend her.

All three of them were on the way to pay a visit to Mary Poppins's uncle, Mr. Wigg, and Jane and Michael had looked forward to the trip for so long that they were more than half afraid that Mr. Wigg might not be in, after all.

"Why is he called Mr. Wigg—does he wear one?" asked Michael, hurrying along beside Mary Poppins.

"He is called Mr. Wigg because Mr. Wigg is his name. And he doesn't wear one. He is bald," said Mary Poppins. "And if I have any more questions we will just go Back Home." And she sniffed her usual sniff of displeasure.

Jane and Michael looked at each other and frowned. And the frown meant: "Don't let's ask her anything else or we'll never get there."

Mary Poppins put her hat straight at the Tobacconist's Shop at the corner. It had one of those curious windows where there seem to be three of you instead of one, so that if you look long enough at them you begin to feel you are not yourself but a whole crowd of somebody else. Mary Poppins sighed with pleasure, however, when she saw three of herself, each wearing a blue coat with silver buttons and a blue hat to match. She thought it was such a lovely sight that she wished there had been a dozen of her or even thirty. The more Mary Poppins the better.

"Come along," she said sternly, as though they had kept *her* waiting. Then they turned the corner and pulled the bell of Number Three, Robertson Road. Jane and Michael could hear it faintly echoing from a long way away and they knew that in one minute, or two at the most, they would be having tea with Mary Poppins's uncle, Mr. Wigg, for the first time ever.

"If he's in, of course," Jane said to Michael in a whisper.

At that moment the door flew open and a thin, watery-looking lady appeared.

"Is he in?" said Michael quickly.

"I'll thank you," said Mary Poppins, giving him a terrible glance, "to let *me* do the talking."

"How do you do, Mrs. Wigg," said Jane politely.

"Mrs. Wigg!" said the thin lady, in a voice even thinner than herself. "How dare you call me Mrs. Wigg? No, thank you! I'm plain Miss Persimmon *and* proud of it. Mrs. Wigg indeed!" She seemed to be quite upset, and they thought Mr. Wigg must be a very odd person if Miss Persimmon was so glad not to be Mrs. Wigg.

"Straight up and first door on the landing," said Miss Persimmon, and she went hurrying away down the passage saying: "Mrs. Wigg indeed!" to herself in a high, thin, outraged voice.

Jane and Michael followed Mary Poppins upstairs. Mary Poppins knocked at the door.

"Come in! Come in! And welcome!" called a loud, cheery voice from inside. Jane's heart was pitter-pattering with excitement.

"He *is* in!" she signaled to Michael with a look.

Mary Poppins opened the door and pushed them in front of her. A large cheerful room lay before them. At one end of it a fire was burning brightly and in the centre stood an enormous table laid for tea—four cups and saucers, piles of bread and butter, crumpets, coconut cakes and a large plum cake with pink icing.

"Well, this is indeed a Pleasure," a huge voice greeted them, and Jane and Michael looked round for its owner. He was nowhere to be seen. The room appeared to be quite empty. Then they heard Mary Poppins saying crossly:

"Oh, Uncle Albert—not *again?* It's not your birthday, is it?"

And as she spoke she looked up at the ceiling. Jane and Michael looked up too and to their surprise saw a round, fat, bald man who was hanging in the air without holding on to anything. Indeed, he appeared to be *sitting* on the air, for his legs were crossed and he had just put down the newspaper which he had been reading when they came in.

"My dear," said Mr. Wigg, smiling down at the children, and looking apologetically at Mary Poppins, "I'm very sorry, but I'm afraid it *is* my birthday."

"Tch, tch, tch!" said Mary Poppins.

"I only remembered last night and there was no time then to send you a postcard asking you to come another day. Very distressing, isn't it?" he said, looking down at Jane and Michael.

"I can see you're rather surprised," said Mr. Wigg. And, indeed, their mouths were so wide open with astonishment that Mr. Wigg, if he had been a little smaller, might almost have fallen into one of them.

"I'd better explain, I think," Mr. Wigg went on calmly. "You see, it's this way. I'm a cheerful sort of man and very disposed to laughter. You wouldn't believe, either of you, the number of things that strike me as being funny. I can laugh at pretty nearly everything, I can."

And with that Mr. Wigg began to bob up and down, shaking with laughter at the thought of his own cheerfulness.

"Uncle Albert!" said Mary Poppins, and Mr. Wigg stopped laughing with a jerk.

"Oh, beg pardon, my dear. Where was I? Oh, yes. Well, the funny thing about me is—all right, Mary, I won't laugh if I can help it!—that whenever my birthday falls on a Friday, well, it's all up with me. Absolutely U.P.," said Mr. Wigg.

"But why—?" began Jane.

"But how—?" began Michael.

"Well, you see, if I laugh on that particular day I become so filled with Laughing Gas that I simply can't keep on the ground. Even if I smile it happens. The first funny thought, and I'm up like a balloon. And until I can think of something serious I can't get down again." Mr. Wigg began to chuckle at that, but he caught sight of Mary Poppins's face and stopped the chuckle, and continued:

"It's awkward, of course, but not unpleasant. Never happens to either of you, I suppose?"

Jane and Michael shook their heads.

"No, I thought not. It seems to be my own special habit. Once, after I'd been to the Circus the night before, I laughed so much that—would you believe it?—I was up here for a whole twelve hours, and couldn't get down till the last stroke of midnight. Then, of course, I came down with a flop because it was Saturday and not my birthday any more. It's rather odd, isn't it? Not to say funny?

"And now here it is Friday again and my birthday, and you two and Mary P. to visit me. Oh, Lordy, Lordy, don't make me laugh, I beg of you—" But although Jane and Michael had done nothing very amusing, except to stare at him in astonishment, Mr. Wigg began to laugh again loudly, and as he laughed he went bouncing and bobbing about in the air, with the newspaper rattling in his hand and his spectacles half on and half off his nose.

He looked so comic, floundering in the air like a great human bubble, clutching at the ceiling sometimes and sometimes at the gas-bracket as he passed it, that Jane and Michael, though they were trying hard to be polite, just couldn't help doing what they did. They laughed. *And* they laughed. They shut their mouths tight to prevent the laughter escaping, but that didn't do any good. And presently they were rolling over and over on the floor, squealing and shrieking with laughter.

"Really!" said Mary Poppins. "Really, *such* behavior!"

"I can't help it, I can't help it!" shrieked Michael as he rolled into the fender. "It's so terribly funny. Oh, Jane, *isn't* it funny?"

Jane did not reply, for a curious thing was happening to her. As she laughed she felt herself growing lighter and lighter, just as though she were being pumped full of air. It was a curious and delicious feeling and it made her want to laugh all the more. And then suddenly, with a bouncing bound, she felt herself jumping through the air. Michael, to his astonishment, saw her go soaring up through the room. With a little bump her head touched the ceiling and then she went bouncing along it till she reached Mr. Wigg.

*"Well!"* said Mr. Wigg, looking very surprised indeed. "Don't tell me it's *your* birthday, too?" Jane shook her head.

"It's not? Then this Laughing Gas must be catching! Hi
—whoa there, look out for the mantelpiece!" This was to
Michael, who had suddenly risen from the floor and was
swooping through the air, roaring with laughter, and just
grazing the china ornaments on the mantelpiece as he
passed. He landed with a bounce right on Mr. Wigg's
knee.

"How do you do," said Mr. Wigg, heartily shaking
Michael by the hand. "I call this really friendly of you—
bless my soul, I do! To come up to me since I couldn't
come down to you—eh?" And then he and Michael
looked at each other and flung back their heads and simply howled with laughter.

"I say," said Mr. Wigg to Jane, as he wiped his eyes.
"You'll be thinking I have the worst manners in the
world. You're standing and you ought to be sitting—a
nice young lady like you. I'm afraid I can't offer you a
chair up here, but I think you'll find the air quite comfortable to sit on. I do."

Jane tried it and found she could sit down quite com-
fortably on the air. She took off her hat and laid it down
beside her and it hung there in space without any support at all.

"That's right," said Mr. Wigg. Then he turned and
looked down at Mary Poppins.

"Well, Mary, we're fixed. And now I can inquire about
*you,* my dear. I must say, I am very glad to welcome you
and my two young friends here today—why, Mary,
you're frowning. I'm afraid you don't approve of—er—
all this."

He waved his hand at Jane and Michael, and said hurriedly:

"I apologize, Mary, my dear. But you know how it is
with me. Still, I must say I never thought my two young
friends here would catch it, really I didn't, Mary! I suppose I should have asked them for another day or tried
to think of something sad or something—"

"Well, I must say," said Mary Poppins primly, "that I

have never in my life seen such a sight. And at your age, Uncle—"

"Mary Poppins, Mary Poppins, do come up!" interrupted Michael. "Think of something funny and you'll find it's quite easy."

"Ah, now do, Mary!" said Mr. Wigg persuasively.

"We're lonely up here without you!" said Jane, and held out her arms towards Mary Poppins. *'Do* think of something funny!"

"Ah, *she* doesn't need to," said Mr. Wigg sighing. "She can come up if she wants to, even without laughing— and she knows it." And he looked mysteriously and secretly at Mary Poppins as she stood down there on the hearth rug.

"Well," said Mary Poppins, "it's all very silly and undignified, but, since you're all up there and don't seem able to get down, I suppose I'd better come up, too."

With that, to the surprise of Jane and Michael, she put her hands down at her sides and without a laugh, without even the faintest glimmer of a smile, she shot up through the air and sat down beside Jane.

"How many times, I should like to know," she said snappily, "have I told you to take off your coat when you come into a hot room?" And she unbuttoned Jane's coat and laid it neatly on the air beside the hat.

"That's right, Mary, that's right," said Mr. Wigg contentedly, as he leaned down and put his spectacles on the mantelpiece. "Now we're all comfortable—"

"There's comfort *and* comfort," sniffed Mary Poppins.

"And we can have tea," Mr. Wigg went on, apparently not noticing her remark. And then a startled look came over his face.

"My goodness!" he said. "How dreadful! I've just realized—that table's down there and we're up here. What *are* we going to do? We're here and it's there. It's an awful tragedy—awful! But oh, it's terribly comic!" And he hid his face in his handkerchief and laughed loudly into it. Jane and Michael, though they did not want to

miss the crumpets and the cakes, couldn't help laughing too, because Mr. Wigg's mirth was so infectious.

Mr. Wigg dried his eyes.

"There's only one thing for it," he said. "We must think of something serious. Something sad, very sad. And then we shall be able to get down. Now—one, two, three! Something *very* sad, mind you!"

They thought and thought, with their chins on their hands.

Michael thought of school, and that one day he would have to go there. But even that seemed funny today and he had to laugh.

Jane thought: "I shall be grown up in another fourteen years!" But that didn't sound sad at all but quite nice and rather funny. She could not help smiling at the thought of herself grown up, with long skirts and a handbag.

"There was my poor old Aunt Emily," thought Mr. Wigg out loud. "She was run over by an omnibus. Sad. Very sad. Unbearably sad. Poor Aunt Emily. But they saved her umbrella. That was funny, wasn't it?" And before he knew where he was, he was heaving and trembling and bursting with laughter at the thought of Aunt Emily's umbrella.

"It's no good," he said, blowing his nose. "I give it up. And my young friends here seem to be no better at sadness than I am. Mary, can't *you* do something? We want our tea."

To this day Jane and Michael cannot be sure of what happened then. All they know for certain is that, as soon as Mr. Wigg had appealed to Mary Poppins, the table below began to wriggle on its legs. Presently it was swaying dangerously, and then with a rattle of china and with cakes lurching off their plates on to the cloth, the table came soaring through the room, gave one graceful turn, and landed beside them so that Mr. Wigg was at its head.

"Good girl!" said Mr. Wigg, smiling proudly upon her. "I knew you'd fix something. Now, will you take the foot of the table and pour out, Mary? And the guests on either side of me. That's the idea," he said, as Michael ran bobbing through the air and sat down on Mr. Wigg's right. Jane was at his left hand. There they were, all together, up in the air and the table between them. Not a single piece of bread and butter or a lump of sugar had been left behind.

Mr. Wigg smiled contentedly.

"It is usual, I think, to begin with bread and butter," he said to Jane and Michael, "but as it's my birthday we will begin the wrong way—which I always think is the *right* way—with the Cake!"

And he cut a large slice for everybody.

"More tea?" he said to Jane. But before she had time to reply there was a quick, sharp knock at the door.

"Come in!" called Mr. Wigg.

The door opened, and there stood Miss Persimmon with a jug of hot water on a tray.

"I thought, Mr. Wigg," she began, looking searchingly round the room, "you'd be wanting some more hot— Well, I never! I simply *never!*" she said, as she caught sight of them all seated on the air round the table. "Such goings on I never did see. In all my born days I never saw such. I'm sure, Mr. Wigg, I always knew *you* were a bit odd. But I've closed my eyes to it—being as how you paid your rent regular. But such behavior as this—having tea in the air with your guests—Mr. Wigg, sir, I'm astonished at you! It's that undignified, and for a gentleman of your age—I never did—"

"But perhaps you will, Miss Persimmon!" said Michael.

"Will what?" said Miss Persimmon haughtily.

"Catch the Laughing Gas, as we did," said Michael.

Miss Persimmon flung back her head scornfully.

"I hope, young man," she retorted, "I have more respect for myself than to go bouncing about in the air like a rubber ball on the end of a bat. I'll stay on my own feet, thank you, or my name's not Amy Persimmon, and —oh dear, oh *dear,* my goodness, oh *DEAR*—what *is* the matter? I can't walk, I'm going, I—oh, help, *HELP!*"

For Miss Persimmon, quite against her will, was off the ground and was stumbling through the air, rolling from side to side like a very thin barrel, balancing the tray in her hand. She was almost weeping with distress as she arrived at the table and put down her jug of hot water.

"Thank you," said Mary Poppins in a calm, very polite voice.

Then Miss Persimmon turned and went wafting down again, murmuring as she went: "So undignified—and me

a well-behaved, steady-going woman. I must see a doctor—"

When she touched the floor she ran hurriedly out of
the room, wringing her hands, and not giving a single
glance backwards.

"So undignified!" they heard her moaning as she shut
the door behind her.

"Her name can't be Amy Persimmon, because she
*didn't* stay on her own feet!" whispered Jane to Michael.

But Mr. Wigg was looking at Mary Poppins—a curious look, half-amused, half-accusing.

"Mary, Mary, you shouldn't—bless my soul, you
shouldn't, Mary. The poor old body will never get over
it. But, oh, my Goodness, didn't she look funny wad-
dling through the air—my Gracious Goodness, but
didn't she?"

And he and Jane and Michael were off again, rolling about the air, clutching their sides and gasping with laughter at the thought of how funny Miss Persimmon had looked.

"Oh dear!" said Michael. "Don't make me laugh any more. I can't stand it! I shall break!"

"Oh, oh, oh!" cried Jane, as she gasped for breath, with her hand over her heart. "Oh, my Gracious, Glorious, Galumphing Goodness!" roared Mr. Wigg, dabbing his eyes with the tail of his coat because he couldn't find his handkerchief.

"IT IS TIME TO GO HOME." Mary Poppins's voice sounded above the roars of laughter like a trumpet.

And suddenly, with a rush, Jane and Michael and Mr. Wigg came down. They landed on the floor with a huge bump, all together. The thought that they would have to go home was the first sad thought of the afternoon, and the moment it was in their minds the Laughing Gas went out of them.

Jane and Michael sighed as they watched Mary Poppins come slowly down the air, carrying Jane's coat and hat.

Mr. Wigg sighed, too. A great, long, heavy sigh.

"Well, isn't that a pity?" he said soberly. "It's very sad that you've got to go home. I never enjoyed an afternoon so much—did you?"

"Never," said Michael sadly, feeling how dull it was to be down on the earth again with no Laughing Gas inside him.

"Never, never," said Jane, as she stood on tiptoe and kissed Mr. Wigg's withered-apple cheeks. "Never, never, never, never . . . !"

They sat on either side of Mary Poppins going home in the Bus. They were both very quiet, thinking over the lovely afternoon. Presently Michael said sleepily to Mary Poppins:

"How often does your Uncle get like that?"

"Like what?" said Mary Poppins sharply, as though Michael had deliberately said something to offend her.

"Well—all bouncy and boundy and laughing and going up in the air."

"Up in the air?" Mary Poppins's voice was high and angry. "What do you mean, pray, up in the air?"

Jane tried to explain.

"Michael means—is your Uncle often full of Laughing Gas, and does he often go rolling and bobbing about on the ceiling when—"

"Rolling and bobbing! What an idea! Rolling and bobbing on the ceiling! You'll be telling me next he's a balloon!" Mary Poppins gave an offended sniff.

"But he did!" said Michael. "We saw him."

"What, roll and bob? How dare you! I'll have you know that my uncle is a sober, honest, hard-working man, and you'll be kind enough to speak of him respectfully. And don't bite your Bus ticket! Roll and bob, indeed—the idea!"

Michael and Jane looked across Mary Poppins at each other. They said nothing, for they had learned that it was better not to argue with Mary Poppins, no matter how odd anything seemed.

But the look that passed between them said: "Is it true or isn't it? About Mr. Wigg. Is Mary Poppins right or are we?"

But there was nobody to give them the right answer.

The Bus roared on, wildly lurching and bounding.

Mary Poppins sat between them, offended and silent, and presently, because they were very tired, they crept closer to her and leaned up against her sides and fell asleep, still wondering. . . .

# Otis Takes Aim

**by Beverly Cleary**
**Illustrated by Louis Darling**

*Otis Spofford is in the mood for some excitement at school. So he's been throwing spitballs in class. "Otis Spofford," warns his teacher, Mrs. Gitler, "if you throw one more spitball, I'll do something that will make you wish you'd never thought of spitballs." Could Otis resist a challenge like that? No way. One juicy spitball later . . .*

Mrs. Gitler said, "I want you to throw spitballs for me."

The class gasped. Throw spitballs! Whoever heard of a teacher asking someone to throw spitballs?

Even Otis was startled. He didn't know what to think, but he wasn't going to let anyone know he was taken off guard. "Sure," he said. "Any special place you want me to throw them?"

"Into the wastebasket," answered Mrs. Gitler. "I want you to sit on a chair and throw spitballs into the basket."

Otis grinned. The idea of sitting in front of the class to shoot spitballs into the wastebasket pleased him.

But Mrs. Gitler said, "Take your paper, the chair, and the basket to the back of the room."

Otis took his time about moving the chair and the wastebasket.

"Quickly, Otis," said the teacher.

"Spitball Spofford," whispered Stewy.

Otis settled himself on the chair and tore off a piece of paper. After chewing it, he threw it into the wastebasket with enough force to make a noise. He was pleased when the whole class turned around to look at him.

"All right, people. There is no need to watch Otis. We all know what he looks like," said Mrs. Gitler, as she took her pitch pipe out of her desk and the class got out its music books.

Otis chewed and threw. At first, the boys and girls peeked over their shoulders at him, but Mrs. Gitler started the singing lesson with a song about a barnyard. The class had so much fun imitating the sounds of different animals that they all lost interest in Otis.

"Moo-moo," went the first row, taking the part of cows. The second row, who took the part of chickens, made such funny cackles that the whole class laughed and Mrs. Gitler had to start the song again.

Otis chewed more and more slowly. His mouth was dry and he began to feel lonesome all by himself at the back of the room. He stopped making spitballs altogether and sat looking out of the window. It had been raining, and drops of sparkling water dripped from the trees. How good they looked!

"Go on with your spitballs, Otis," Mrs. Gitler re-

minded him at the end of the song. Then she started the class on *Row, Row, Row,* which was one of their favorites.

Otis tore off another piece of paper. He took his time rolling it, because he did not feel much like making a spitball. He put it in his mouth and chewed very, very slowly. He tried counting to ten between each chew. His mouth felt drier and drier, and he decided he hated the taste of paper.

"Row, row, row your boat," sang the class.

Otis sighed. He did not want to give up and admit to Mrs. Gitler that he had had enough of spitballs. Not in front of the whole class.

"Gently down the stream," sang the class.

Gently down the stream, thought Otis. Why did everything have to make him think of water? Doggedly he kept at his spitballs, but he worked as slowly as he could. He was wondering how he could make his spit last until school was out. He ran his tongue around his mouth. Then he stuck it out as far as he could to see if it were swelling up and turning black. He could barely see the tip, which was still pink. That was a good sign. Maybe he could hold out.

"Merrily, merrily, merrily," trilled the class.

Suddenly the fire-drill bell rang. He was saved! Otis leaped from his chair and was first in line at the door. If only he could get to a drinking fountain, he knew he could make his spit last until school was out.

"Quickly, children," said Mrs. Gitler. "Get in line. Don't push, George. Come along, Austine."

As soon as the class was lined up two by two, Mrs. Gitler opened the door and marched the boys and girls rapidly through the hall and down the stairs. She walked beside Otis, who looked longingly at the drinking fountain as they passed. With Mrs. Gitler beside him, there was no way he could get to it. The more he thought about that drinking fountain, the drier his mouth felt. If he could just turn the handle and let the cool water flow into his mouth for one instant!

Outdoors, the air was cool and damp. Otis opened his mouth and drew in gasps of cool air. He didn't care if he looked like a goldfish.

"Spitball Spofford," the boys and girls whispered to him as he opened his mouth toward the sky in case it should begin to rain again.

When everyone was out of the building, the bell rang again. "All right, class, about face," ordered Mrs. Gitler.

The class turned. This left Otis and his partner at the end of the line instead of the beginning. Now it would be easier to get to the drinking fountain. As soon as the class reached the top of the stairs, Otis bent over so Mrs. Gitler would not see him and darted behind the line of boys and girls to the fountain. He turned the handle, and just as the stream of water rose almost to his mouth, he felt a hand on his shoulder. It was the principal. "You know that no one is supposed to leave his line during a fire drill," said Mr. Howe, and steered Otis back to his place in line.

If that isn't my luck, thought Otis. Now my spit will never last.

As the class entered the room again, Otis was tempted to go back to his seat and hope Mrs. Gitler would forget the whole thing. But he knew that if he did Stewy or Linda or someone else would probably remind her. Anyway, he was not going to give in until he had to. He returned to his chair at the back of the room and tore off another piece of paper. Mrs. Gitler ignored him. Slowly he chewed the spitball and pitched it into the wastebasket. He tore off another piece of paper and looked at the clock. Another hour to chew and throw. A long, long hour. A minute clicked by and after a long time, another.

Otis put the paper in his mouth but he did not chew it. He just held it there a minute and took it out again. He never wanted to taste paper again. Mrs. Gitler had won. He only hoped she would not find it out.

The teacher looked up from her desk. "Well, Otis?" she asked.

Otis tried to lick his lips, but his mouth was too dry. "I guess . . . I guess . . . I've run out of spit," he said.

"Are you sure you're through throwing spitballs?" Mrs. Gitler wanted to know.

Otis did not want to answer the question, but he had to. "Yes," he said in a small voice.

"You may go out and get a drink before you return to your seat." Mrs. Gitler's eyes twinkled and she looked as if she wanted to laugh.

Otis managed a sheepish halfway grin as he went out of the room. Then he ran down the hall to the drinking fountain. How wonderful the jet of cold water looked! He drank in great gulps, stopped to gasp for breath, and gulped some more. Never had anything tasted so good. Otis drank for a long time before he wiped his mouth on his sleeve. He drank for such a long time that Mrs. Gitler came out into the hall to see what had happened to him.

"Was making me throw spitballs my comeuppance?" Otis wanted to know.

Mrs. Gitler laughed. "It would be for some boys, but I'm not sure about you." Then she shook her head. "Otis, if only you would work as hard on your spelling as you do on mischief!"

"Aw . . ." muttered Otis, because he couldn't think of anything else to say.

Back at his desk, Otis found the class was no longer interested in what he had done. As far as they were concerned, the excitement was over. He also discovered that although he was no longer thirsty, he still had a funny taste in his mouth from chewing so much paper. As he worked at his spelling, it began to bother him more and more. He wished he had something to eat that would take away the awful papery taste.

He fished through his pockets to see what he could find. Maybe he had an old stick of gum or something. In among his rabbit's foot, yo-yo, and rubber bands, Otis's fingers found the bud of garlic he had grabbed from the kitchen that morning. He untangled it and looked at it. He wondered what it would taste like. He smelled it and decided it smelled bad and good at the same time. Hold-

ing it under his desk, he pulled off a section and peeled off the pinkish outside skin. He popped it into his mouth, bit, and for a terrible instant was sorry. Tears came to his eyes, his nose tingled, and he blew the air out of his mouth.

Instantly everyone sitting near him turned to look at him. Ellen wrinkled her nose. Austine held hers.

"Wow!" whispered Stewy. "What's that awful smell?"

*Wow* is right, thought Otis, as he gulped and blew again. He bit into the garlic once more. The second bite was not quite so bad as the first. Almost, but not quite. Trying to look as if he ate raw garlic all the time, he chewed a couple of times and blew again.

"Otis Spofford," Ellen said in a fierce whisper, "you stop that!"

Otis grinned. This was just what he wanted. Things were back to normal. He took a deep breath and blew as hard as he could at Ellen.

# THE SNOOKS FAMILY
## by Harcourt Williams

*The Snooks are silly folks who'll make you laugh. After you read their story, tell it to your friends until they make you stop!*

One night Mr. and Mrs. Snooks were going to bed as usual. It so happened that Mrs. Snooks got into bed first, and she said to her husband, "Please, Mr. Snooks, would you blow the candle out?"

And Mr. Snooks replied, "Certainly, Mrs. Snooks." Whereupon he picked up the candlestick and began to blow, but unfortunately he could only blow by putting his under lip over his upper lip, which meant that his breath went up to the ceiling instead of blowing out the candle flame.

And he puffed and he puffed and he puffed, but he could not blow it out.

So Mrs. Snooks said, "I will do it, my dear," and she got out of bed and took the candlestick from her husband and began to blow. But unfortunately she could only blow by putting her upper lip over her under lip, so that all her breath went down onto the floor. And she puffed and she puffed, but she could not blow the candle out.

So Mrs. Snooks called their son John. John put on his sky-blue dressing gown and slipped his feet into his primrose-colored slippers and came down into his parents' bedroom.

"John, dear," said Mrs. Snooks, "will you please blow out the candle for us?"

And John said, "Certainly, Mummy."

But unfortunately John could only blow out of the right corner of his mouth, so that all his breath hit the wall of the room instead of the candle.

And he puffed and he puffed, but he could not blow out the candle.

So they all called for his sister, little Ann. And little Ann put on her scarlet dressing gown and slipped on her pink slippers and came down to her parents' bedroom.

"Ann, dear," said Mr. Snooks, "will you please blow the candle out for us?"

And Ann said, "Certainly, Daddy."

But unfortunately Ann could only blow out of the left side of her mouth, so that all her breath hit the wall instead of the candle.

And she puffed and she puffed and she puffed, but she could not blow out the candle.

It was just then that they heard in the street below a heavy, steady tread coming along the pavement. Mr. Snooks threw open the window and they all craned their heads out. They saw a policeman coming slowly towards the house.

"Oh, Mr. Policeman," said Mrs. Snooks, "will you come up and blow out our candle? We do so want to go to bed."

"Certainly, Madam," replied the policeman, and he entered and climbed the stairs—*blump, blump, blump.* He came into the bedroom where Mr. Snooks, Mrs. Snooks, John Snooks and little Ann Snooks were standing around the candle which they could NOT blow out.

The policeman then picked up the candlestick in a very dignified manner and, putting his mouth into the

usual shape for blowing, puffed out the candle at the first puff. Just like this—PUFF!

Then the Snooks family all said, "Thank you, Mr. Policeman."

And the policeman said, "Don't mention it," and turned to go down the stairs again.

"Just a moment, Policeman," said Mr. Snooks. "You mustn't go down the stairs in the dark. You might fall." And taking a box of matches, he LIT THE CANDLE AGAIN!

Mr. Snooks went down the stairs with the policeman and saw him out the door. His footsteps went *blump, blump, blump* along the quiet street.

John Snooks and little Ann Snooks went back to bed. Mr. and Mrs. Snooks got into bed again. There was silence for a moment.

"Mr. Snooks," said Mrs. Snooks, "would you blow out the candle?"

Mr. Snooks got out of bed. "Certainly, Mrs. Snooks," he said . . .

And so on AD INFINITUM....

# Dribble!

**by Judy Blume**
**Illustrated by Roy Doty**

*Peter Hatcher, age nine, won his pet turtle, Dribble, at a birthday party. Peter has a lock and chain on his bedroom door to protect Dribble from his three-year-old brother, Fudge. But it takes more than locks and chains to keep Fudge in line.*

I will never forget Friday, May tenth. It's the most important day of my life. It didn't start out that way. It started out ordinary. I went to school. I ate my lunch. I had gym. And then I walked home from school with Jimmy Fargo. We planned to meet at our special rock in the park as soon as we changed our clothes.

In the elevator I told Henry I was glad summer was coming. Henry said he was too. When I got out at my floor I walked down the hall and opened the door to my apartment. I took off my jacket and hung it in the closet. I put my books on the hall table next to my mother's purse. I went straight to my room to change my clothes and check Dribble.

The first thing I noticed was my chain latch. It was unhooked. My bedroom door was open. And there was a chair smack in the middle of my doorway. I nearly tumbled over it. I ran to my dresser to check Dribble. He wasn't there! His bowl with the rocks and water was there—but Dribble was gone.

I got really scared. I thought, *Maybe he died while I was at school and I didn't know about it.* So I rushed into the kitchen and hollered, "Mom . . . where's Dribble?" My mother was baking something. My brother sat on the kitchen floor, banging pots and pans together. "Be quiet!" I yelled at Fudge. "I can't hear anything with all that noise."

"What did you say, Peter?" my mother asked me.

"I said I can't find Dribble. Where is he?"

"You mean he's not in his bowl?" my mother asked.

I shook my head.

"Oh dear!" my mother said. "I hope he's not crawling around somewhere. You know I don't like the way he smells. I'm going to have a look in the bedrooms. You check in here, Peter."

My mother hurried off. I looked at my brother. He was smiling. "Fudge, do you know where Dribble is?" I asked calmly.

Fudge kept smiling.

"Did you take him? Did you, Fudge?" I asked not so calmly.

Fudge giggled and covered his mouth with his hands.

I yelled. "Where is he? What did you do with my turtle?"

No answer from Fudge. He banged his pots and pans together again. I yanked the pots out of his hand. I tried to speak softly. "Now tell me where Dribble is. Just tell me where my turtle is. I won't be mad if you tell me. Come on, Fudge . . . please."

Fudge looked up at me. "In tummy," he said.

"What do you mean, in tummy?" I asked, narrowing my eyes.

"Dribble in tummy!" He repeated.

"What tummy?" I shouted at my brother.

"This one," Fudge said, rubbing his stomach. "Dribble in this tummy! Right here!"

I decided to go along with his game. "Okay. How did he get in there, Fudge?" I asked.

Fudge stood up. He jumped up and down and sang out, "I ATE HIM . . . ATE HIM . . . ATE HIM!" Then he ran out of the room.

My mother came back into the kitchen. "Well, I just can't find him anywhere," she said. "I looked in all the dresser drawers and the bathroom cabinets and the shower and the tub and . . ."

"Mom," I said, shaking my head. "How could you?"

"How could I what, Peter?" Mom asked.

"How could you let him do it?"

"Let who do what, Peter?" Mom asked.

"LET FUDGE EAT DRIBBLE!" I screamed.

My mother started to mix whatever she was baking. "Don't be silly, Peter," she said. "Dribble is a turtle."

"HE ATE DRIBBLE!" I insisted.

*"Peter Warren Hatcher!* STOP SAYING THAT!" Mom hollered.

"Well, ask him. Go ahead and ask him," I told her.

Fudge was standing in the kitchen doorway with a big grin on his face. My mother picked him up and patted his head. "Fudgie," she said to him, "tell Mommy where brother's turtle is."

"In tummy," Fudge said.

"What tummy?" Mom asked.

"MINE!" Fudge laughed.

My mother put Fudge down on the kitchen counter where he couldn't get away from her. "Oh, you're fooling Mommy . . . right?"

"No fool!" Fudge said.

My mother turned very pale. "You really ate your brother's turtle?"

Big smile from Fudge.

"YOU MEAN THAT YOU PUT HIM IN YOUR MOUTH AND CHEWED HIM UP . . . LIKE THIS?" Mom made believe she was chewing.

"No," Fudge said.

A smile of relief crossed my mother's face. "Of course you didn't. It's just a joke." She put Fudge down on the floor and gave me a *look.*

Fudge babbled. "No chew. No chew. Gulp . . . gulp . . . all gone turtle. Down Fudge's tummy."

Me and my mother stared at Fudge.

"You didn't!" Mom said.

"Did so!" Fudge said.

"No!" Mom shouted.

"Yes!" Fudge shouted back.

"Yes?" Mom asked weakly, holding onto a chair with both hands.

"Yes!" Fudge beamed.

My mother moaned and picked up my brother. "Oh no! My angel! My precious little baby! OH . . . NO . . ."

My mother didn't stop to think about my turtle. She didn't even give Dribble a thought. She didn't even stop to wonder how my turtle liked being swallowed by my brother. She ran to the phone with Fudge tucked under one arm. I followed. Mom dialed the operator and cried, "Oh help! This is an emergency. My baby ate a turtle . . . STOP THAT LAUGHING," my mother told the operator. "Send an ambulance right away—25 West 68th Street."

Mom hung up. She didn't look too well. Tears were running down her face. She put Fudge down on the floor. I couldn't understand why she was so upset. Fudge seemed just fine.

"Help me, Peter," Mom begged. "Get me blankets."

I ran into my brother's room. I grabbed two blankets from Fudge's bed. He was following me around with that silly grin on his face. I felt like giving him a pinch. How could he stand there looking so happy when he had my turtle inside him?

I delivered the blankets to my mother. She wrapped Fudge up in them and ran to the front door. I followed and grabbed her purse from the hall table. I figured she'd be glad I thought of that.

Out in the hall I pressed the elevator buzzer. We had to wait a few minutes. Mom paced up and down in front of the elevator. Fudge was cradled in her arms. He sucked his fingers and made that slurping noise I like. But all I could think of was Dribble.

Finally, the elevator got to our floor. There were three people in it besides Henry. "This is an emergency," Mom wailed. "The ambulance is waiting downstairs. Please hurry!"

"Yes, Mrs. Hatcher. Of course," Henry said. "I'll run her down just as fast as I can. No other stops."

Someone poked me in the back. I turned around. It was Mrs. Rudder. "What's the matter?" she whispered.

"It's my brother," I whispered back. "He ate my turtle."

Mrs. Rudder whispered *that* to the man next to her and *he* whispered it to the lady next to *him* who whispered it to Henry. I faced front and pretended I didn't hear anything.

My mother turned around with Fudge in her arms and said, "That's not funny. Not funny at all!"

But Fudge said, "Funny, funny, funny Fudgie!"

Everybody laughed. Everybody except my mother.

The elevator door opened. Two men, dressed in white, were waiting with a stretcher. "This the baby?" one of them asked.

"Yes. Yes, it is," Mom sobbed.

"Don't worry, lady. We'll be to the hospital in no time."

"Come, Peter," my mother said, tugging at my sleeve. "We're going to ride in the ambulance with Fudge."

My mother and I climbed into the back of the blue ambulance. I was never in one before. It was neat. Fudge kneeled on a cot and peered out through the window. He waved at the crowd of people that had gathered on the sidewalk.

One of the attendants sat in back with us. The other one was driving. "What seems to be the trouble, lady?" the attendant asked. "This kid looks pretty healthy to me."

"He swallowed a turtle," my mother whispered.

"He did WHAT?" the attendant asked.

"Ate my turtle. That's what!" I told him.

My mother covered her face with her hanky and started to cry again.

"Hey, Joe!" the attendant called to the driver. "Make it snappy . . . *this* one swallowed a turtle!"

"That's not funny!" Mom insisted. I didn't think so either, considering it was my turtle!

We arrived at the back door of the hospital. Fudge was whisked away by two nurses. My mother ran after him. "You wait here, young man," another nurse called to me, pointing to a bench.

I sat down on the hard, wooden bench. I didn't have anything to do. There weren't any books or magazines spread out, like when I go to Dr. Cone's office. So I watched the clock and read all the signs on the walls. I found out I was in the emergency section of the hospital.

After a while the nurse came back. She gave me some paper and crayons. "Here you are. Be a good boy and draw some pictures. Your mother will be out soon."

I wondered if she knew about Dribble and that's why she was trying to be nice to me. I didn't feel like drawing any pictures. I wondered what they were doing to Fudge in there. Maybe he wasn't such a bad little guy after all. I remembered that Jimmy Fargo's little cousin once swallowed the most valuable rock from Jimmy's collection. And my mother told me that when I was a little kid I swallowed a quarter. Still . . . a quarter's not like a turtle!

I watched the clock on the wall for an hour and ten minutes. Then a door opened and my mother stepped out with Dr. Cone. I was surprised to see him. I didn't know he worked in the hospital.

"Hello, Peter," he said.

"Hello, Dr. Cone. Did you get my turtle?"

"Not yet, Peter," he said. "But I do have something to show you. Here are some X-rays of your brother."

I studied the X-rays as Dr. Cone pointed things out to me.

"You see," he said. "There's your turtle . . . right there."

I looked hard. "Will Dribble be in there forever?" I asked.

"No. Definitely not! We'll get him out. We gave Fudge some medicine already. That should do the trick nicely."

"What kind of medicine?" I asked. "What trick?"

"Castor oil, Peter," my mother said. "Fudge took castor oil. And milk of magnesia. And prune juice too. Lots of that. All those things will help to get Dribble out of Fudge's tummy."

"We just have to wait," Dr. Cone said. "Probably until tomorrow or the day after. Fudge will have to spend the night here. But I don't think he's going to be swallowing anything that he isn't supposed to be swallowing from now on."

"How about Dribble?" I asked. "Will Dribble be all right?" My mother and Dr. Cone looked at each other. I knew the answer before he shook his head and said, "I think you may have to get a new turtle, Peter."

"I don't want a new turtle!" I said. Tears came to my

eyes. I was embarrassed and wiped them away with the back of my hand. Then my nose started to run and I had to sniffle. "I want Dribble," I said. "That's the only turtle I want."

My mother took me home in a taxi. She told me my father was on his way to the hospital to be with Fudge. When we got home she made me lamb chops for dinner, but I wasn't very hungry. My father came home late that night. I was still up. My father looked gloomy. He whispered to my mother, "Not yet . . . nothing yet."

The next day was Saturday. No school. I spent the whole day in the hospital waiting room. There were plenty of people around. And magazines and books too. It wasn't like the hard bench in the emergency hallway. It was more like a living room. I told everybody that my brother ate my turtle. They looked at me kind of funny. But nobody ever said they were sorry to hear about my turtle. Never once.

My mother joined me for supper in the hospital coffee shop. I ordered a hamburger but I left most of it. Because right in the middle of supper my mother told me that if the medicine didn't work soon Fudge might have to have an operation to get Dribble out of him. My mother didn't eat anything.

That night my grandmother came to stay with me. My mother and father stayed at the hospital with Fudge. Things were pretty dreary at home. Every hour the phone rang. It was my mother calling from the hospital with a report.

"Not yet . . . I see," Grandma repeated. "Nothing happening yet."

I was miserable. I was lonely. Grandma didn't notice. I even missed Fudge banging his pots and pans together. In the middle of the night the phone rang again. It woke me up and I crept out into the hallway to hear what was going on.

Grandma shouted, "Whoopee! It's out! Good news at last."

She hung up and turned to me. "The medicine has finally worked, Peter. All that castor oil and milk of magnesia and prune juice finally worked. The turtle is out!"

"Alive or dead?" I asked.

"PETER WARREN HATCHER. WHAT A QUESTION!" Grandma shouted.

So my brother no longer had a turtle inside of him. And I no longer had a turtle! I didn't like Fudge as much as I thought I did before the phone rang.

# The Tongue-twister

**by B. Wiseman**

*Do you want to see how angry a moose can make a bear? Read this story about Morris and Boris, two surprisingly good friends.*

"Can you say a tongue-twister?" Boris asked.

Morris said, "A tongue-twister."

"That is just the name of it," Boris said. "What you must say is: Peter Piper picked a peck of pickled peppers."

Morris asked, "What is a peck?"

Boris said, "A peck is a lot of something. Go on, say it."

Morris said, "A peck is a lot of something."

"No! No!" Boris cried. "Say the whole thing!"

Morris said, "The whole thing."

"No! No! NO!" Boris shouted. "Say: Peter Piper picked a peck of pickled peppers!"

Morris asked, "What are pickled peppers?"

Boris said, "Come with me . . . These are peppers. Pickled peppers are peppers you put in a pot and pickle. To pickle means to make sour. Now say the tongue-twister."

Morris said, "Peter Piper picked a peck of peppers and put them in a pot and pickled them."

"NO!" Boris cried. "Peter Piper picked a peck of pick-led peppers!"

Morris asked, "How could Peter Piper pick a peck of pickled peppers? Pickled peppers are peppers you put in a pot and pickle!"

"I KNOW THAT!" Boris shouted. "But in the tongue-twister, Peter Pepper . . ."

Morris said, "You mean Peter Piper."

"YES!" Boris yelled. "Peter Piper! In the tongue-twister, Peter Piper pecked a pick . . ."

Morris cried, "You mean picked a peck!"

"YES! YES!" Boris roared. "Picked a peck! In the tongue-twister, Peter Piper picked a peck of pickled pots! No! I mean Peter Piper picked a pot of pickled pecks! No! No! Oh, you got me all mixed up! You will never learn to say a tongue-twister!"

And Boris went away.

A bird asked Morris, "Why was Boris yelling?"

Morris said, "Because I could not say: Peter Piper picked a peck of pickled peppers."

**5**

ROW, ROW, ROW YOUR GOAT

Funny Poems

## Young Lady, Whose Nose

There is a young lady, whose nose,
Continually prospers and grows;
   When it grew out of sight,
   She exclaimed in a fright,
"Oh! Farewell to the end of my nose!"

*Edward Lear*

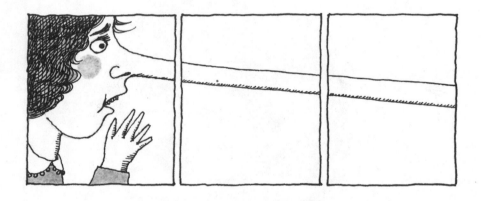

## Young Lady of Spain

There was a young lady of Spain
Who was dreadfully sick on a train,
   Not once, but again
   And again and again,
And again and again and again.

*Author Unknown*

## Old Man from Peru

There was an old man from Peru
Who dreamed he was eating his shoe.
In the midst of the night
He awoke in a fright
And found it was perfectly true!

*Author Unknown*

## Old Man with a Beard

There was an Old Man with a beard
Who said, "It is just as I feared!
Two Owls and a Hen
Four Larks and a Wren
Have all built their nests in my beard!"

*Edward Lear*

# Double Meanings

## Wild Flowers

"Of what are you afraid, my child?" inquired
the kindly teacher.
"Oh, sir! the flowers, they are wild,"
replied the timid creature.

*Peter Newell*

## Puzzling

Here's a fact that will cause you to frown—
Instead of growing up, a goose grows down!

*William Cole*

## Night, Knight

"Night, night,"
said one knight
to the other knight
the other night.
"Night, night, knight."

*Author Unknown*

## Rhododendron, of Course

A major, with wonderful force,
Called out in Hyde Park for a horse.
All the flowers looked round,
But no horse could be found,
So he just rhododendron, of course.

*Author Unknown*

## Two Elephants

Two elephants went to the pool one day,
But the lifeguard there made them go away.
He said their swimsuits would never do,
For they only had one pair of trunks for two.

*Madeleine Edmondson*

# Little Willie Rhymes

Willie poisoned Auntie's tea.
Auntie died in agony.
Uncle came and looked quite vexed.
"Really, Will," said he, "what next?"

*Author Unknown*

Little Willie hung his teacher.
Hung so high, they couldn't reach her.
They called mother in to school.
"Willie broke another rule."

*Stephanie Calmenson and Joanna Cole*

Willie sawed a man in two.
Couldn't put him back with glue.
Said Mother as she mopped the floors,
"Can't you play these games outdoors?"

*Stephanie Calmenson and Joanna Cole*

Willie, in one of his nice new sashes,
Fell in the fire and was burnt to ashes.
Now, although the room grows chilly,
We haven't the heart to poke poor Willie.

*Author Unknown*

# Goops and Other Folks

### The Goops

The Goops they lick their fingers,
    And the Goops they lick their knives;
They spill their broth on the tablecloth—
    Oh, they lead disgusting lives!
The Goops they talk while eating,
    And loud and fast they chew;
And that is why I'm glad that I
    Am not a Goop—are you?

*Gelett Burgess*

### Speak Roughly to Your Little Boy

Speak roughly to your little boy,
    And beat him when he sneezes:
He only does it to annoy,
    Because he knows it teases.

*Lewis Carroll*

## A Dirty Old Man

"Who are you?"
"A dirty old man;
I've always been so
Since the day I began.
Father and Mother
Were dirty before me,
Hot or cold water
Has never come o'er me."

*English Nursery Rhyme*

## My Face

As a beauty I am not a star,
There are others more handsome,
    by far,
    But my face—I don't mind it
    For I am behind it.
It's the people in front get the jar!

*Anthony Euwer*

252

**WHAT'S FOR DINNER?**

SOMETHING GOOD, I HOPE.

**Through the Teeth**

Through the teeth
And past the gums.
Look out, stomach,
Here it comes!

*Traditional*

**Oyster Stew**

An oyster met an oyster
And they were oysters two;
Two oysters met two oysters
And they were oysters too;
Four oysters met a pint of milk,
And they were oyster stew!

*Gyles Brandreth*

### The Catsup Bottle

Shake and shake
the catsup bottle.
None will come
and then a lot'll.

*Richard Armour*

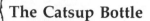

### Hot Dog

My father owns the butcher shop.
My mother cuts the meat.
And I'm the little hot dog
That runs around the street.

*Traditional*

### Celery

Celery, raw,
Develops the jaw.
But celery, stewed,
Is more quietly chewed.

*Ogden Nash*

## Never Take a Pig to Lunch

Never take a pig to lunch
Don't invite him home for brunch
Cancel chances to be fed
Till you're certain he's well-bred.

Quiz him! Can he use a spoon?
Does his sipping sing a tune?
Will he slurp and burp and snuff
Till his gurgling makes you gruff?

Would he wrap a napkin 'round
Where the dribbled gravy's found?
Tidbits nibble? Doughnut dunk?
Spill his milk before it's drunk?

Root and snoot through soup du jour?
Can your appetite endure?
If his manners make you moan
Better let him lunch alone.

*Susan Alton Schmeltz*

## Boa Constrictor

Oh I'm being eaten by a boa constrictor,
A boa constrictor, a boa constrictor,
I'm being eaten by a boa constrictor,
And I don't like it . . . one bit!
Well what do you know . . . it's nibbling my toe,
Oh gee . . . it's up to my knee,
Oh my . . . it's up to my thigh,
Oh fiddle . . . it's up to my middle,
Oh heck . . . it's up to my neck,
Oh dread . . . it's . . . MMFFF.

*Shel Silverstein*
from *Where the Sidewalk Ends*

## The Frog

What a wonderful bird the frog are—
When he stand, he sit almost
When he hop, he fly almost
He ain't got no sense hardly
He ain't got no tail hardly either
When he sit, he sit on what he ain't got almost!

*Author Unknown*

## Hippopotamus

See the handsome hippopotamus,
Wading on the river-bottomus.
He goes everywhere he wishes
In pursuit of little fishes.
Cooks them in his cooking-potamus.
"My," fish say, "he eats a lot-of-us!"

*Joanna Cole*

## Perils of Thinking

A centipede was happy quite,
    Until a frog in fun
Said, "Pray, which leg comes after which?"
This raised her mind to such a pitch,
She lay distracted in the ditch
    Considering how to run.

*Author Unknown*

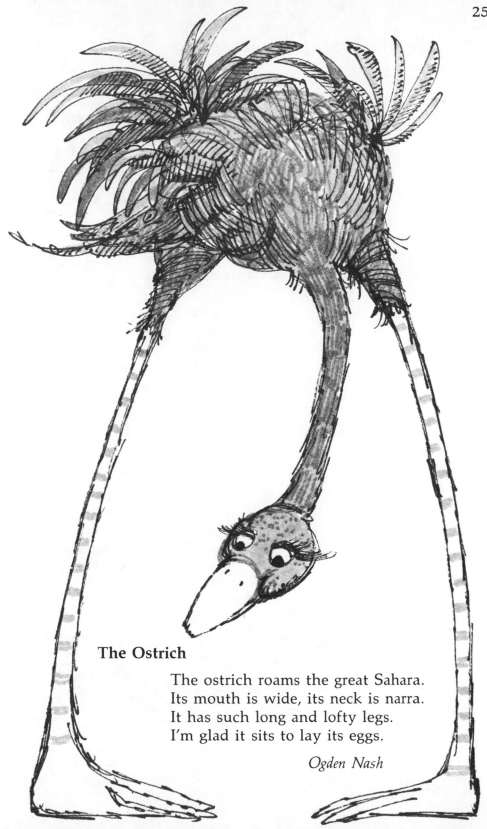

### The Ostrich

The ostrich roams the great Sahara.
Its mouth is wide, its neck is narra.
It has such long and lofty legs.
I'm glad it sits to lay its eggs.

*Ogden Nash*

# Eight Teasing Rhymes . . .

Marguerite, go wash your feet.
The Board of Health's across the street.

I saw you in the ocean.
I saw you in the sea.
I saw you in the bathtub.
Oops, pardon me!

Here comes the bride
Big, fat, and wide.
Here comes the groom
Stiff as a broom.

I see London,
I see France,
I see someone's
Underpants.

Cry, baby, cry,
Stick your finger in your eye
And tell your mother
It wasn't I.

Liar, liar
Your pants are on fire.
Your nose is as long
As a telephone wire.

Two's a couple
Three's a crowd
Four on the sidewalk's
Not allowed.

Melissa is so small
A rat could eat her, hat and all.

## And One Answer for All

Sticks and stones will break my bones
But names will never hurt me.

*Traditional*

NONSENSE POEMS

### Jabberwocky

'Twas brillig, and the slithy toves
   Did gyre and gimble in the wabe:
All mimsy were the borogoves,
   And the mome raths outgrabe.

"Beware the Jabberwock, my son!
   The jaws that bite, the claws that catch!
Beware the Jubjub bird, and shun
   The frumious Bandersnatch!"

He took his vorpal sword in hand:
   Long time the manxome foe he sought—
So rested he by the Tumtum tree,
   And stood awhile in thought.

And, as in uffish thought he stood,
   The Jabberwock, with eyes of flame,
Came whiffling through the tulgey wood,
   And burbled as it came!

One, two! One, two! And through and through
  The vorpal blade went snicker-snack!
He left it dead, and with its head
  He went galumphing back.

"And hast though slain the Jabberwock?
  Come to my arms, my beamish boy!
O frabjous day! Callooh! Callay!"
  He chortled in his joy.

'Twas brillig, and the slithy toves
  Did gyre and gimble in the wabe:
All mimsy were the borogoves,
  And the mome raths outgrabe.

*Lewis Carroll*

## Mairzy Doats

Mairzy doats and dozy doats
And liddle lamzy divey;
A kiddley divey too,
Wouldn't you?

(Mares eat oats and does eat oats
And little lambs eat ivy;
A kid'll eat ivy too,
Wouldn't you?)

*Milton Drake, Al Hoffman,*
*and Jerry Livingston*

## Did You Eever, Iver, Over?

Did you eever, iver, over
In your leef, life, loaf
See the deevel, divel, dovel
Kiss his weef, wife, woaf?

No, I neever, niver, nover
In my leef, life, loaf,
Saw the deevel, divel, dovel
Kiss his weef, wife, woaf.

*Traditional*

# Hand-Clapping Rhyme

**Miss Lucy**

Miss Lucy had a baby.
She named him Tiny Tim.
She put him in the bathtub
To see if he could swim.

He drank up all the water.
He ate up all the soap.
He tried to eat the bathtub,
But it wouldn't go down his throat.

Miss Lucy called the Doctor.
Miss Lucy called the Nurse.
Miss Lucy called the Lady
With the alligator purse.

In walked the Doctor.
In walked the Nurse.
In walked the Lady
With the alligator purse.

"Measles," said the Doctor.
"Chicken Pox," said the Nurse.
"Mumps," said the Lady
With the alligator purse.

Out walked the Doctor.
Out walked the Nurse.
Out walked the Lady
With the alligator purse.

*Traditional*

# Mother Goose?

### Twinkle, Twinkle, Little Bat

Twinkle, twinkle, little bat!
How I wonder what you're at!
Up above the world you fly,
Like a tea tray in the sky.

*Lewis Carroll*

## Row, Row, Row Your Goat

Row, row, row your goat
Gently down the stream.
Merrily, merrily, merrily, merrily,
Life is just a scream.

*Stephanie Calmenson*

## Little Miss Tuckett

Little Miss Tuckett
Sat on a bucket,
Eating some peaches and cream.
There came a grasshopper
And tried hard to stop her,
But she said, "Go way, or I'll scream."

*Author Unknown*

## Say Dis with D's

### The Penny in the Gum Slot

*First say the poem this way:*

I put the penny in the gum slot.
You saw the gum come down.
You get the wrapper.
I get the gum.
'Cause I put the penny in the gum slot.

*Now say the same poem but begin every word
with the letter D:*

Die dut de denny din de dum dot.
Doo daw de dum dum down.
Doo det de dapper.
Die det de dum.
Dause die dut de denny din de dum dot.

*Now say it again as fast as you can. Try it on a friend.*

*Author Unknown*

**Yours Till the Kitchen Sinks**

**6**

Go little album far and near
To all my friends I hold so dear.
And ask them each to write a page
That I may read in my old age.

Roses are red.
Violets are blue.
I'm so handsome.
What happened to you?

Sweethearts in a hammock
Ready to kiss.
All of a sudden
It goes like this.

When you get married
And live in a tree
Send me a coconut
C.O.D.

Two in the car.
Two little kisses.
Two weeks later
Mr. and Mrs.

Round went the album
Hither it came
For me to write
So here's my name.

Little Jack Horner sat in a corner
Watching Louella go by.
He thought her a beauty
And said, "Come here, cutie."
That's how he got his black eye.

Humpty Dumpty sat on a wall
Humpty Dumpty had a great fall.
All the king's horses and all the king's men
Had scrambled eggs for breakfast again.

Tell me fast before I faint
Is we friends, or is we ain't?

Never kiss
By the garden gate.
Love is blind
But the neighbors ain't.

Oh, this page of whitey-white.
It looked so good, I took a bite.

Can't think
Brain numb
Inspiration
Won't come.
Bad ink
Worse pen
Best wishes
Amen.

Remember Grant,
Remember Lee.
But most of all
Remember ME.

U R 2 Nice
2 B 4 Gotten

I am a nut.
I am a clown.
That's why I signed here
Upside down.

Dot
Blot
Forget-me-not.

Henry ate a hot dog.
His eyes rolled up above.
Henry ate a dozen more
And died of puppy love.

Ellen had a little bear
To which she was so kind.
And everywhere that Ellen went
She had her bear behind.

May your life be like toilet paper—
long and useful.

Just a few lines to remember me by.

May your life be like spaghetti—
long and full of dough.

Yours till the ocean waves.

Yours till day breaks.

Yours till night falls.

Yours till Cats-kill Mountains.

Yours till the ocean wears
rubber pants to keep its bottom dry.

Yours till cereal bowls.

Yours till the pencil case is solved.

Yours till lemon drops.

Yours till the kitchen sinks.

Yours till Bear Mountain gets dressed.

Yours till lip-sticks.

Yours till potato chips.

# Newsbreaks

**by Charles Keller**

A boat carrying a shipment of Yo-Yos across the ocean sprang a leak and sank fifty times.

Because of a strike at the cemetery, gravedigging will be done by a skeleton crew.

Two hundred hares escaped from a rabbit farm; police are combing the area.

# Best Sellers
# (Books You'll Never Read)

**by Stephanie Calmenson**

*It's a Dog's Life* by Ima Mongrel
*Overcoming Your Fears* by R. U. Yellow
*The Private Eye's Handbook* by Hugh Dunnit
*How to Get Your Work Done Faster* by Sheik Alleg
*Weather Trends for the Future* by Hugh Nose
*True Love* by I. M. Yaws
*Beating the Blues* by Watts D. Matter, M.D.
*How to Weight-lift a Brick Building* by Noah Kandoo
*I Work for Peanuts* by Ella Fant
*By the Dawn's Early Light* by Jose Canusi
*Fix It, Dear Liza* by Holin D. Buckit

# Weather Report

## by Judi Barrett

*And now here is the weather report from the town of Chewand-swallow, where residents eat whatever comes from the sky:*

Lamb chops, becoming heavy at times, with occasional ketchup. Periods of peas and baked potatoes followed by gradual clearing, with a wonderful Jell-O setting in the west.

Tomorrow, cloudy with a chance of meatballs.

# How to Get a Dog

**by Delia Ephron**

Tell your parents that you want a dog more than anything in this world. Promise that you'll take care of it. Cross your heart and hope to die. They won't have to do a thing. You'll walk it and feed it. Please. Please. Pretty-please. Pretty-please with sugar on top. Pretty-please with whipped cream and a cherry. Please, Mom, please. You are, too, old enough. When they say that you have to wait one more year, stamp your foot. Scream, "You never trust me; you never believe me. Why don't you trust me?"

Run to your room, slam the door, open the door, and yell, "It's not fair." Slam the door again. When your mother comes to your room, have the following conversation:

"That's enough," says she.

Say, "All right," as though it isn't.

"I said,.'That's enough.' "

"All I said was 'All right.' "

"It's not what you said, it's how you said it."

"Okay, Mom, but . . ."

and repeat entire scene from "I want a dog more than anything in the world" to "Why don't you trust me?" Convince her.

When your mother says that it's time to feed the dog, say, "Just a second." When she says it's time to walk the dog, say, "In a minute." After she reminds you again, tell her that you just want to watch the end of the TV show. Then take out the dog, complaining that it's so boring to walk it and besides you can't find the leash. Use your belt instead.

Each day, procrastinate and complain until your mother finds it easier to feed it and walk it herself.

# How to Be the Perfect Host

**by Pat Relf**

*You say you're thinking of having a party? Here are some tips you'll want to keep in mind:*

The key to a successful party is *planning.* Your invitations must be sent to your guests well ahead of time. If the party is to be a formal affair, let your guests know what to wear by saying, "Make sure to wear an undershirt" or "Please paint your feet."

As your party draws near, make sure that your home is spanking clean. Remember: a place for everything and everything in its place, and when the place gets too crowded, there's always room under the bed. (By the way, you might want to hide that fungus farm of yours in your sock drawer. It will be safe there.)

Always take particular care in dressing. Your attire sets the tone for the evening. The perfectly groomed host knows that there's nothing like a tasteful anchovy bow tie to spice up an otherwise dull evening costume.

Thoughtful guests will bring their host a small gift, such as rubber bands or gravel. You will, of course, want to put the gravel in water at once. Don't forget to say, "Thank you very much. I just *love* gravel," even if you prefer mud or shredded paper.

Hang up your guests' coats neatly, taking special care not to wrinkle or dirty them. If an accident occurs, and you spill purple ink on a guest's coat, remember: salt, flour, concentrated orange juice, and a little more ink will remove the stain.

Proper introductions are essential to any successful social gathering. Be certain everyone at your party meets everyone else.

It is correct to introduce a four-headed monster in a clockwise direction, starting with the head closest to you. Upon being introduced yourself, say, "How do you do?" and shake hands. Shaking hands with a chicken poses a difficult problem. Our advice is to wing it.

# You Can't Eat Peanuts in Church and Other Little-known Laws

**by Barbara Seuling**

*All these are real laws that are now or have been on the books!*

In Tahoe City, California, cowbells may not be worn by horses.

In San Francisco, you are forbidden by law to spit on your laundry.

In Idaho, you cannot buy a chicken after dark without the sheriff's permission.

In Wyoming, it is illegal to take a picture of a rabbit during January, February, March, or April—unless you have a license.

In New York, it is unlawful to disturb the occupant of a house by ringing the doorbell.

It is illegal to eat peanuts in church in Massachusetts.

Barbers in Hawaii are not permitted to lather the chins of their customers with a shaving brush.

In Baltimore, Maryland, it is against the law to mistreat an oyster.

# The Frog Speaker

## by Mike Thaler

## That's Life!

"Comedy must be real and true to life. When things get bad enough, they become funny."
*Charlie Chaplin*

## Alexander and the Terrible, Horrible, No Good, Very Bad Day

**by Judith Viorst**

I went to sleep with gum in my mouth and now there's gum in my hair and when I got out of bed this morning I tripped on the skateboard and by mistake I dropped my sweater in the sink while the water was running and I could tell it was going to be a terrible, horrible, no good, very bad day.

I think I'll move to Australia.

## Murphy's Laws

**by Arthur Bloch**

Law of reruns: If you have watched a TV series only once, and watch it again, it will be a rerun of the same episode.

Law of finding things: You can always find what you're not looking for.

Cole's Law: Thinly sliced cabbage.

# The Doctor Is In

## by Charles M. Schulz

# McProverbs
## by Sid Fleischman

It's more blessed to give than to receive—unless you have chicken pox.

Don't follow the crowd. Everyone may be going to the dentist.

When success goes to someone's head, it generally finds nothing there.

Never try to take a bone away from a dog unless it's an ankle bone—yours.

Birds of a feather that flock together make a good target.

Never trust the arithmetic of a man who must take off his shoes to count to twenty.

Haste makes wastepaper.

It's good luck to find a penny. It's better luck to find a ten-dollar bill.

# McBroom's Painless Cold Remedy

### by Sid Fleischman

To cure the common cold make a tonic of the following ingredients: six parsnips, eleven onions, a pint of molasses, three gallons of rainwater, a dill pickle, and the head of a mackerel. Simmer on top of the stove for seven days, then make a dozen brownies.

By this time your cold will be gone, and you won't have to take the tonic. But you will be hungry. Eat the brownies.

# Solutions

### Solution to This is a Test . . . on page 82–83:

You read the sign, didn't you?
Don't worry, no one passes this test!

### Solution to the Rebus on pages 96–97:

## The Tale of Jason and the Three Wishes

Once Jason's mother and father sent their son to visit his Aunt Rose. But the very first night, he began to look pale. His voice was hoarse. He sneezed, "A-shoo."

Aunt Rose called the doctor, who said, "Put him to bed. Give him this medicine. He'll soon be well."

Lying in bed was not fun. Jason was bored. Suddenly he heard a noise. The door was ajar. Someone had come in. Who could it be?

Jason looked around and saw a tiny elf. The elf was drinking Jason's medicine.

"Hey, I need that medicine," said Jason.

"I love pink medicine," said the elf.

"Give it back!" yelled Jason.

"It's all gone," said the elf, "but I'll give you three wishes instead. Then you can wish to be well."

The elf waved goodbye.

Jason wished to feel greater than he ever had before, and at once he did. Then he said, "I wish I could fly." And this wish came true too.

Jason began to swing his arms. He jumped out the window and flew for blocks and blocks. When he came back, Aunt Rose was staring at the empty bed.

"Watch me fly," said Jason.

But Aunt Rose grabbed him. "You can forget about flying!" she cried.

"I wish we *could* forget it . . ." began Jason.

That was the third wish. It came true. So they both forgot about flying forever.

Of course, Jason can still fly if he tries to but nobody knows that—except the elf.

**Solutions to Penny Puzzles on page 98–99:**

1. Solution: Put the bottom penny on top of the middle one.

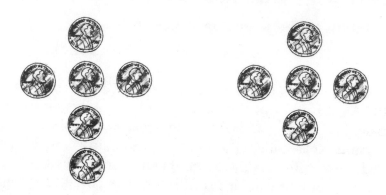

2. Solution: Take the end pennies on the bottom row and place them on either end of the second row. Then take the top penny and put it at the bottom.

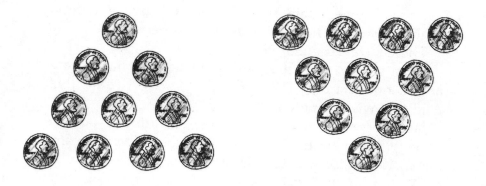

**Solutions to Matchstick Puzzles on page 100:**

1. Solution:

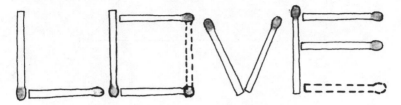

2. Solution: Move one match to leave a small square opening in the center.

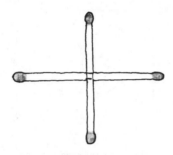

3. Solution:

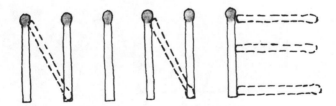

**Solution to Grunchies on page 102:**

The first and the third monsters are Grunchies. (All Grunchies have four pointed teeth.)

**Solution to Write 100 on page 103:**

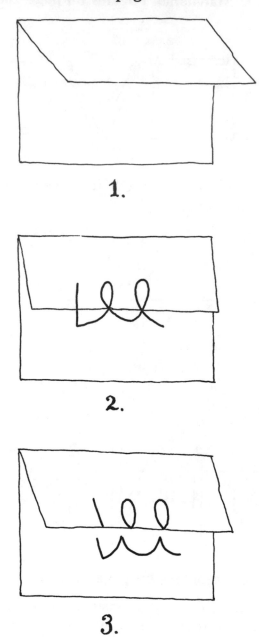

1.

2.

3.

**Solutions to Secret Codes on page 104:**

Number Code: Good
Backward Code: This is spelled backward.
Add-Three Code: You are pretty smart!

# Index

**Joanna Cole** has taught elementary school, has worked for a newsmagazine, and for several years was a senior editor for children's books. Today, she is a full-time author, writing for and about children. Many of her more than two dozen children's books have been selected by the American Library Association as Notable Books. She compiled two anthologies, *A New Treasury of Children's Poetry* and *Best-Loved Folktales of the World.* She is married, has a daughter, Rachel, and lives in New York City.

**Stephanie Calmenson** is the author of numerous books for children, including *The Kindergarten Book* and *The After School Book.* Before turning to writing full time, she was an elementary school teacher, a children's book editor, and Editorial Director of Parents Magazine's Read Aloud Book Club for Children. She grew up in Brooklyn, New York and now lives in Manhattan.

**Marylin Hafner,** an illustrator of more than twenty-five books for children, is a contributing artist for *Cricket* magazine and a designer of rubber stamps and greeting cards. She studied at Pratt Institute, Brooklyn, and the School of Visual Arts in Manhattan. She is the mother of three daughters and lives in Cambridge, Massachusetts.